Are We Free Yet?

TINA STRAWN

Are We Free Yet?

The Black Queer Guide
to Divorcing America

RHI

Library of Congress Cataloging-in-Publication Data Available Upon Request
ISBN 978-1-955905-05-3 (TP)
ISBN 978-1-955905-11-4 (eBook)
Printed in the United States
Distributed by Simon & Schuster

Book design by Aubrey Khan, Neuwirth & Associates, Inc.
Bird by Diego Naive from NounProject.com

First edition
10 9 8 7 6 5 4 3 2 1

In loving memory of Breonna Taylor and Erica Watson.

I wish we were all hippies and did yoga, lived in cottages, smoked weed, accepted everyone for who they are, and listened to wonderful music. I wish money didn't make us who we are. I just wish we could redo society.

—UNKNOWN

Table of Contents

The Guide to the Guide . . . . *xv*

PART I
Grief and Healing

1. The United Shades of Black Grief *3*
2. The Threat of Black Death *5*
3. Just Mercy *10*
4. Activist Timeline *12*
5. It Began in Shorter, Alabama *13*
6. Get Therapy *16*
   ARTIFACT: *Excerpt from "Honoring the Ori: Mindfulness Meditation at the Intersection of Black Women's Spirituality and Sexualities"*
7. Black Suffering *21*
8. False Allyship *23*
9. One Nation under Black Trauma *26*
   ARTIFACT: *Emmett Till Antilynching Act*
10. A Black American Horror Story from Texas *31*
11. Find Stillness Every Day through Breath *34*
12. Reaching the (Housing) Limit of Racialized Trauma *37*
    ARTIFACT: *"Healing Racial Trauma with Dr. Candice Nicole Hargons"*

13. Heartbreak Is a Gray Grief for Activists 44
    A Poem on Separation and Surviving

14. Reparations and Black Bereavement Time 48
    ARTIFACT: *Commission to Study and Develop Reparation*
        Proposals for African Americans Act

15. Grief Is Intergenerational 54

16. Grieving Is the Starting Point to Getting Free 58

17. Find Movement Every Day 60

18. Sit with Your Anger 62
    A Poem about Kindness and Anger

19. Run Away 65

20. Make Space to Grieve 67

21. From Broken Hearts to Divorces 68
    A Poem about Serenity

22. Gather Your Spiritual Practices 71
    ARTIFACT: *The Eight Limbs of Yoga*

23. Reclaim Your Time 74
    ARTIFACT: *Grieving and Healing Playlist*

PART II
Peace and Pleasure

24. The Envelope in the Door 79

25. Unpack Your Relationship with Anti-Blackness 81

26. Unpack Your Relationship with Capitalism 83

27. Unpack Your Relationship with Credit 86

28. Learn about Rent Strikes 89

29. Create Radical Strategies for
    Your Own Personal Liberation 91

30. Let Go: Aparigraha 93

31. Nomad AF 95

32. Finding Peace in Pain 97

33. Protect Your Peace at All Costs *100*

34. Unplug from the Virtual and Digital Chaos *102*

35. Make Peace with Your Past *103*

36. Get Outside *106*

37. WPP (White People's Problem) *107*

38. Team Blaxit *109*

39. Black Americans Who Moved Abroad *111*

40. Welcome to Jamrock *114*
     A Poem about Privilege, Passports, and Wedding Rings

41. Unpack Your Relationship with Patriarchy *118*

42. Learn about Misogynoir and Intersectionality *120*

43. Build Your Community *121*

44. Get Queer AF *123*

45. Breaking Out of Cis-heteronormativity *126*
     A Poem about Sexual (R)Evolution

46. Unpack Your Relationship with Sexual Pleasure *130*

47. Have Interstellar Sex *131*

48. Increase Your Pleasure Capacity: Have More Orgasms . . . *133*
     A Poem about Coconuts and Beaches

49. Pleasure Power Principles *140*

50. Take a Nap *142*
     ARTIFACT: *Peace and Pleasure Playlist*

PART III

Celebration and Joy

51. A Brief History of Black Celebration *147*

52. Find Your Voice *148*
     ARTIFACT: *"Lift Every Voice and Sing"*

53. Eat *150*
     ARTIFACT: *Ingredients from a Jamaican Menu*

54. Yoga Meals *153*

55. Comments Overheard While Eating in Costa Rica *155*

56. Soul Food Stories *156*
ARTIFACT: *Variations on Beans and Rice*

57. The War on Drugs *159*
ARTIFACT: *Three Acts That Weaponized Weed against Black Americans*

58. Cannabis as Liberation *162*

59. Get High *165*

60. Draw Your Pleasure Treasure Map *167*
ARTIFACT: *Weed Playlist*

61. Get into Your Body *169*

62. Dance *171*

63. Honor All the Parts of Yourself, Then and Now *172*

64. Forgiveness *174*
A Poem about Dust

65. Rename Yourself *176*

66. Be Gracious *178*

67. Find Restorative "Poetic" Justice *179*

68. Queer Black Sheep *181*
ARTIFACT: *Queer Morning Blessings*

69. Follow Your Joy *184*

70. My Solo Poly Honeymoon *185*

71. The Pleasure and Politics of Polyamory *189*

72. Take Risks *192*
A Poem about Risk

73. Create Your Own Constitution of Joy *194*
ARTIFACT: *AWFY Joy and Celebration Playlist*

PART IV
Activism and Liberation

74. The Case for Divorcing America *199*

75. Meeting Stacey Abrams *200*

76. Evaluate Your Relationship with the Democratic Party . . . *203*

77. To Vote or Not to Vote *205*

78. Losing the Black Woman's Vote *208*

79. Grumpy Old White Men *211*

80. Satan or Lucifer *213*

81. Science, History, Medicine, and Time *215*

82. Radical Theory #1 . . . . *217*

83. Unvaccinated Black Lives Matter Too *219*

84. If I Die of COVID-19
     (or Any Other Natural Black Disaster) *221*
     A Poem about Fear

85. Loving Erica *224*

86. One Love *226*
     A Poem about Last Night

87. Losing Erica *229*
     ARTIFACT: *Last Text Messages from Erica*
     A Poem about Jamaica

88. Alive *234*

89. Being a Liberation Activist *236*

90. Write Your Own Declaration of Liberation *238*

91. White People for Black Lives: Educate Yourself *240*

92. White People, Take Action *242*

93. I Am Not Your Resource *244*

94. The Liberation of Mutual Aid *245*

95. Poor People Shit *248*

96. Never Stop Listening to
    and Learning from Black Women *251*
    ARTIFACT: *Excerpts from the Combahee River
    Collective Statement*

97. Closure *254*

98. Saying Goodbye *257*

99. Dear America *259*

100. What Hope *261*
    ARTIFACT: *Activism and Liberation Playlist*

Acknowledgments *263*

*References for "Honoring the Ori: Mindfulness Meditation
at the Intersection of Black Women's Spirituality and
Sexualities" by Natalie Malone and Candice N. Hargons* *265*

Tina's Bibliography *267*

About the Author *269*

The Guide to the Guide

———————

I have a deep knowing, an ancestral calling, and a burning desire that my life's purpose is to speak, teach, write, and travel. In the summer of 2019, I retired from my fifteen-year fitness career to do just that, all focused on my antiracism work of educating, facilitating, coaching, consulting, and podcasting. I was a part of a newish community of antiracism educators and racial justice activists, advocates, allies, accomplices, and coconspirators all committed to fighting systemic racism and dismantling white supremacy in the United States. All of us were committed to the fight for Black lives. We were a part of the new civil rights movement. We were the revolution, and we were gonna change the world.

Thanks to COVID-19, by March 2020, the revolution went virtual and digital. When I reflect back on some of the collective traumas we experienced that year, in addition to living through a global pandemic, I think about and hold with great tenderness the murders of Ahmaud Arbery, Breonna Taylor, George Floyd, and too many other Black lives that were taken so brutally, senselessly, and rapidly that we didn't seem to have time to catch our grief breaths before there was another Black life taken, another Black name turned into a hashtag. Black America was under attack in a very visible and viral way. We were constantly being fed horrific images and videos of Black trauma porn. The country was thick and sick with the stench of Black death. By the time summer rolled around, and the country started to burn with uprisings in the streets, this activist was completely burnt the fuck out.

But let's run this back a bit . . .

I became comfortable with calling myself an activist in 2017, "activated" in a political sense in November 2016. I attended the Women's March of January 2017 in Atlanta, and after getting connected with several local, online, liberal, and Democratic groups (made up of predominantly white women), I got my first taste of politics. I started phone banking, canvassing, writing postcards, and reaching out to my local government representatives in an attempt to make my voice heard. In the work and on the streets, I met John Lewis and Jon Ossoff, Lucy McBath, Cory Booker, and other Democratic candidates, elected officials, and shining stars. I was a poll watcher for several local elections and received training from the LBGTQ+ rights organization Georgia Equality on holding voter registration drives, and I personally scheduled, organized, and hosted a dozen voter registration events across the Atlanta area during the 2018 midterm election season. I volunteered on a few political campaigns, including those of Stacey Abrams for governor of Georgia—the first Black woman to represent a national party for governor of any US state—and another local Black woman who was running for a house district seat in my very white, affluent, and conservative community of East Cobb, in the city of Marietta.

While I was getting politically involved, I was also continuing my journey of racial awakening, a journey that had begun in July 2016 after I accidentally saw the videos on Facebook of Alton Sterling and Philando Castile being killed by cops, which both shattered me and radicalized me. Being so broken by the racial realities with which I was forced to reckon, I began doing the deep inner work of unpacking my own internalized racism, which led me to develop a meditation practice, something I didn't have despite the fact that I had been teaching yoga classes in many studios and boutiques since 2012. I then started protesting and marching in the streets. I read *Just Mercy*, a memoir by the lawyer and social justice activist Bryan Stevenson, which had such a tremendous impact on me that I created antiracism and yoga trips, which are designed for folx who are on their own personal antiracism journeys and want to use the practice and philosophy of yoga as tools to dismantle racism. I was invited to speak on panels about racism and white supremacy, and I was volunteering at local high schools, speaking with their gay-straight alliance groups.

By the fall of 2019, I had twice been a guest on *Speaking of Racism*, a newly formed podcast by a white Midwestern woman named Jen Kinney. As a result of those podcast episodes, I began to get emails from white women around the country asking me for antiracism coaching and for more information about Legacy Trips. My antiracism work was growing.

As the exposure of the podcast and social media platform grew, Jen faced tough and valid concerns from Black women questioning her role as a white woman owning a podcast that talked about racism. This led her to ask me to acquire the podcast, making it Black led and Black owned.

So going into January 2020, I was the new owner of the *Speaking of Racism* podcast, and scheduled to host more Legacy Trips and more screenings and discussions of HBO's documentary *True Justice: Bryan Stevenson's Fight for Equality*. And I planned to do more traveling, together with my wife, as nomads around the globe. At the top of the year that likely changed the shape of our species, my own life took a turn for the unexpected.

I've embarked on a radical personal journey toward freedom—and it is at this point in the story that I invite you to get interactive with me. Because this is where this memoir turns into a guidebook, one aimed at helping you find your own answer to the question I have been asking myself since early 2020: "Are we free yet?"

Throughout these pages, I will offer opportunities for you to reflect on what your personal journey toward freedom has looked like and continues to look like. Because that is what I did that led me here.

The thing that qualifies me to write about freedom is my own personal search for liberation. A letter in the door alerting my wife and me to an upcoming foreclosure of the house we were renting started me on this path to figuring out radical ways of getting free from oppressive systems. I didn't know it at the time, but I was becoming a liberation activist.

If you are searching for what freedom looks like and feels like for you, then you also are becoming a liberation activist. That's what qualifies us. That's it.

As you read this book, you'll find that I've provided opportunities, pit stops in the form of AWFY artifacts, activities, and journal prompts, for you to do some evaluating. The purpose of this is to locate YOU at these different moments of both the specific national events and moments in your own personal life, so you can follow your own liberation journey road map, while reading along with mine.

Here are a few things you'll need to work through this guidebook:

- an AWFY journal (anything that works for writing or taking notes)

- something to stream music on (playlists will be provided)

- a hefty supply of tissues (for tears)

- a vibrator or other sex toy as you feel comfortable using one (or other object, item, or consenting adult that will help bring you sexual pleasure)

- a joint or a blunt if you use weed to get high

- water, always water

- curiosity, imagination, and an open heart and mind

Are We Free Yet? is written through my lens as a queer, Black, currently woman-identified, minimalist nomad, with an ex-husband and an ex-wife, and a country that I am divorcing. In fact, I am writing and editing the final pages of the book from my studio apartment that I rent and have lived in for the past six months in Atenas, Costa Rica. I've written this book on divorcing America because that's what I'm in the process of doing.

And I'm not the only one.

As someone who is interested in reading my words, you are likely interested in learning about radical and queer ways to get free.

Excellent. Welcome. I've been expecting you.

PART

I

Grief
and
Healing

ONE

The United Shades
of Black Grief

I n early 2020, the assault against Black life in the US at the hands of the state was at an all-time high. From my perspective as a queer Black American woman who had been a full-time nomad with my wife since February 1, 2020, in many ways, the first several months of 2020 felt like a peak of anti-Black violence. Black death due to white supremacy was increasingly common while remaining consistently terrorizing. At the time, I was greatly anticipating getting out of the United States, though with the arrival of COVID-19 in March 2020, the work that I had previously secured in Durban, South Africa, was canceled. Since that had been my ticket out of the States, I wasn't exactly sure how I was going to leave the country.

With the new global pandemic, our ability (as Americans with the coveted blue passport) to travel when and where we wanted to changed. As we formulated a strategy to leave, we continued to watch the bodies of Black people pile up around the nation of red, white, and blue.

- On February 23, 2020, Ahmaud Arbery, a young Black man, was murdered by three white men in Georgia. His killers were arrested almost three months later, only after a video of them chasing him down and shooting him went viral, sparking worldwide outrage. They were ultimately found guilty of murder in November 2021.

- On March 5, 2020, the state of Alabama executed Nathaniel Woods, a forty-three-year-old Black man, for being an accomplice to murders committed by someone else.

- On March 13, 2020, Breonna Taylor, a young Black woman, was shot in her home while she slept by a SWAT team in Kentucky. No one was ever held accountable for her death.

The day after Nate Woods was executed, I wrote on my Instagram account, "We are not safe and we are not free. They are still lynching us. If you are able, please consider RAGE donating today to the Equal Justice Initiative or to the Innocence Project. Today we lament. Today we hold space for the family and friends of Nathaniel Woods. Tomorrow, we burn this system down."

Early evening, the day of Nate's scheduled execution, there had been reports that he had been granted a stay of execution. On social media, there was starting to be relief that they were not going to execute him. However, despite the fact that the Alabama Supreme Court had recommended a stay, Alabama governor Kay Ivey did not grant it, and since she did not intervene, the state proceeded with the execution.

On Facebook, there was a live link from the local newspaper that was updating a tragic countdown timeline of what was happening to Nate . . . *At 3 p.m., Nate is transferred from his cell, he says his goodbyes, offers his last words, he goes into the execution chamber, he is murdered by the state.*

I logged off the internet and just lost it. I went to bed that night holding on to a thread of invisible hope that they were not going to execute him, that there would be some miracle breakthrough in the final moments. But when I woke up the next morning, the sun was peeking at me through the drawn hotel curtain in Johns Creek, Georgia, where my wife, Dawn, and I had arrived a few days earlier. A bird was chirping unusually loudly outside my window, as if to tell me that Nate was now free. I realized that they did kill him, and I was broken all over again.

TWO

The Threat of
Black Death

When someone Black is killed by white supremacy, and the news of the death circulates online, the grief is felt and shared on a cultural level across the Black diaspora. Just as we Black folx experience oppression at a deeper level systemically (consider the disproportionate rate at which Black folx are incarcerated, or the maternal mortality rate, which is much higher for Black women than for women of other racial groups), we also share a particular kind of Black grief, which is deeper than ordinary grief, both energetically and ancestrally. Whether it is the death of a beloved Black actor, celebrity, or public figure, or someone that we heard was killed by police for some unfounded, illogical, and fear-based reason, we share in a collective loss.

By creating art, writing songs, or explaining how we had things in common with the newly deceased, we empathize, seeing our brothers and sisters and cousins and parents and aunties and uncles in every Black death. Just like Black kids at predominantly white schools, just like the universal Black head nod, just like the not-so-mysterious ways that Black people can describe what would happen to you as a child if you responded to an elder by saying, "What?" instead of "Ma'am?" or "Sir?"

For example, all Black Americans can explain what we were doing when we learned that Trayvon Martin was killed, how we heard about it, and what we felt. We can go into detail about what it brought up for us because there is a Trayvon in all our families. Likewise, from what we know about whiteness, there is always a George Zimmerman who will be found not guilty of killing us in a US court of law. It was Trayvon's murderer's acquittal that inspired three queer Black women—Alicia Garza, Patrisse Cullors, and Opal Tometi—to create the mantra that sparked a movement across the globe in 2013: Black Lives Matter.

But BLM goes beyond the narrow nationalism that can be prevalent within Black communities, which merely calls on Black people to love Black, live Black, and buy Black, keeping straight cis Black men at the front of the movement while our sisters, queer and trans siblings, and disabled folx take up roles in the background or not at all. Black Lives Matter affirms the lives of all Black queer and trans folx, disabled folx, undocumented folx, folx with records, women, and all Black lives along the gender spectrum. It centers those that have been marginalized within Black liberation movements. It is a tactic to (re)build the Black liberation movement. When we say Black Lives Matter, we are broadening the conversation around state violence to include all the ways in which Black people are intentionally left powerless at the hands of the state. We are talking about the ways in which Black lives are deprived of our basic human rights and dignity. These were sourced from a now-deleted page on the official Black Lives Matter website (www.blacklivesmatter.com), original author unknown:

- Black poverty and genocide are state violence.

- The 2.8 million Black people locked in cages in this country is state violence.

- Black women bearing the burden of a relentless assault on our children and our families is state violence.

- Black queer and trans folks bear a unique burden from a heteropatriarchal society that disposes of us like garbage and simultaneously fetishizes us and profits off us, and that is state violence.

- Five hundred thousand Black people in the US are undocumented immigrants and relegated to the shadows, which is state violence.

- Black girls are used as negotiating chips during times of conflict and war. This is state violence.

- Black folks living with disabilities and different abilities bear the burden of state-sponsored Darwinian experiments that attempt to squeeze us into boxes of normalcy as defined by white supremacy, which is state violence.

The nation grew more and more desensitized to Black death as we were exposed to more and more Black trauma porn with the click of a button and a scroll on our handheld devices. Our names were turned into hashtags splattered like bloodstains across the World Wide Web. Social media campaigns denouncing the anti-Black violence would start in honor of the deceased Black individual. Videos from dash and body cams and bystanders with cameras on their phones capturing the final moments of a Black person's life became commonplace on social media newsfeeds among the posts about restaurants we ate at and pictures of our pets.

With every viral video of Black death, with every hashtag, with every BLM profile picture frame or black square, Black folx in America grew wearier and wearier.

What I felt after Nate's execution was another shade of the same Black grief. When I dropped my wife off at work that morning after, I couldn't get myself together, so I sat in the parking lot of her job for hours, trying to console myself. I didn't respond to text messages or emails. I would eventually cancel all my meetings for the day and didn't do anything on my to-do list. I wept. I yelled and cussed. I ranted angrily on Facebook Live. I was heartbroken. Again. The devastation I felt when Alabama killed another Black man caught me off guard and consumed me. I realized that my grief over the grave injustice of executing Nate was about more than just Nate. It was about the ever-growing number of Black folx killed, lynched, and publicly executed by police and America's refusal to acknowledge and take accountability for and reconcile its continual history of anti-Black violence and terror. It was about our whole Black community and our collective trauma.

Our tears shed over senseless state-sanctioned killings symbolize the Black blood that has been spilled at public lynchings held on courthouse lawns after Reconstruction, or in backwoods that moved into courtrooms during Jim Crow.

All of us sense the sting of the loss of another Black life. Perhaps it is the ghost sting of the whip used by slave masters to torture enslaved Africans in front of the other enslaved people for the purpose of sending an implicit warning, a terrorist ransom note, a reminder for all of us to stay in line. That sting is the threat felt, again, in every Black life and death to which this nation denies justice.

Sometimes we would argue on our social media posts with white folx who contended that police killings weren't a race issue. Sometimes our sadness boiled over into strongly worded responses to ignorant white coworkers who complained about NFL players kneeling during the national anthem. Sometimes we wouldn't, couldn't, engage the denial and cognitive dissonance because the emotional labor involved in trying to get white people to understand what they were committed to misunderstanding was beyond exhausting, as well as re-traumatizing. It was as though the "All Lives Matter" white folx arguing with us on social media believed that whatever they had learned about racism in America in elementary school during Black History Month was all the education on race they needed. The national message to the rest of the world from the House of Whiteness seemed to be a rationalization that since slavery had ended, and since we had had a Black president for eight years, we were living in something called a "post-racial society."

Black folx knew this to be just one of many "great white lies" told by our imperialist, colonized nation, accounting for why our deaths and murders continued to demonstrate the lack of "justice for all" that the Pledge of Allegiance arrogantly and mistakenly boasted.

America is still remarkably confused about how to end the senseless violence against Black people at the hands of everyday police officers. The demands from Black activists and leaders to "defund the police" continue to perplex and elude cities and counties across the country, and abolition strategies around ending policing and the prison industrial complex continue to be seen as radical and bizarre. The "inevitability of error" argument made in response to the percentage of innocent people (overwhelmingly Black people) put to death by the death penalty is further proof of a nation that is unable and unwilling to end the anti-Black violence. The idea that error is inherent to the justice system, and therefore acts of injustice are malignant and not intended, has led to many Black deaths being written off as procedural, instead of criminal.

For Black people, knowing all the details surrounding these deaths by police means facing the reality that our skin color is a criminalizing factor. And even as details come out, the community is often resigned to the low likelihood that anyone will be held accountable for killing us, or that anything of substance will be done to prevent our senseless deaths from happening again. If there were to be justice for all, that would look like Black lives not being taken consistently and recklessly by the police state. But America has never had justice in mind for us, as solidified in the very founding documents that birthed the nation, allegedly granting liberty and justice for "all" while making the distinction that our enslaved African ancestors were only three-fifths of a human being.

Justice continues to escape us to this day.

THREE

Just Mercy

I n early 2018, I read the book *Just Mercy* by civil rights lawyer Bryan Stevenson, which had a tremendous impact on me. I was stunned to discover how unjustly the US criminal justice system was operating in the twenty-first century. The stories of the people Stevenson represented, who had been wrongfully accused of crimes and sentenced to life in prison or even death row, were eye-opening. The type of injustice Stevenson describes in his book seemed from another time. Were we still in the era of Jim Crow? The more I read and learned about the work of Stevenson and the Equal Justice Initiative (EJI), the more I realized there were a lot of untold truths that our nation seemed to not want Americans, or the rest of the world, to know or care about.

In April 2018, the EJI opened the National Memorial for Peace and Justice and the Legacy Museum: From Enslavement to Mass Incarceration in Montgomery, Alabama. After making a discovery trip there in October of that year, I felt strongly that everyone, all Americans, should go to this memorial and museum to face the truth of this part of American history. I felt that white allies in particular should have important conversations about what they saw there instead of what I imagined them doing, which was walking through the memorial and museum, nodding respectfully, and then going to Applebee's afterward without taking the time or the space to process what they had learned and felt, or to identify and strategize about how to incorporate and integrate antiracism principles and accountability in their everyday lives. I felt there needed to be a space where people on their own antiracism journey could turn their awareness of how racism and white supremacy continued to operate in our nation into a plan to take action toward being the change they want to see in the world. It was there, after I had walked under the pillars inscribed with the names of known and unknown Black victims of terror lynchings across all fifty states, where my mind, heart, and ancestral guidance began to conjure up something . . .

While continuing my own personal journey of unpacking my Black identity and the ways that I had assimilated into whiteness after a lifetime of thinking that we were elevated from racism as a modern nation, I felt led by my own inner voice, by Spirit, and by the ancestors to create an opportunity for people on their own antiracism journeys to visit these sites in Montgomery, Alabama. And so I started three-day antiracism and yoga trips to the lynching memorial and the Legacy Museum, where we utilized the practice and philosophy of yoga as tools to dismantle racism. In December 2018, I led my first trip.

In 2019, I led five more of these trips and by the fall of that year, I had changed the name from Satya Yoga Trips to Legacy Trips. And while Legacy is the name of the EJI museum that we visit on all our trips, I actually selected the name "Legacy Trips" from Mother Maya Angelou's words, "Your legacy is every life you've touched."

After I created Legacy Trips, Alabama began suffocating me. There is so much historical significance in Alabama, the backdrop of so many events during the civil rights movements of the 1950s and 1960s: Montgomery, Selma, Birmingham. The state felt as toxic as its murky waters where our ancestors drowned, where slave ships arrived to sell Black humans in the square in the center of downtown Montgomery, which we walked past on our way to the Legacy Museum. The drive to and through Alabama still carries the ghosts of the freedom fighters who were killed, and the ghosts of their killers. And they are still killing us.

I decided that for my own sanity and mental health, I personally could not continue going back and forth to Alabama every other month leading groups of white people through this Black history pilgrimage, a decision that led me to partner with several other Black antiracism educators from other parts of the country to facilitate the trips.

FOUR

Activist Timeline

Consider your own "activist" timeline and write it out in your journal.

Here are some things to consider: What does being an activist mean to you? What activated you? What (or who) radicalized you? Write about what your activism has looked like since your defining moment. Where did you take that first step? Where do you want your liberation staircase to lead you?

Start at your moment of realization and go forward from there to here and now.

Maybe this is the very beginning of your activist journey; that's exactly what this handbook is for. We'll walk through many actions together. You can begin right now.

FIVE

It Began in Shorter, Alabama

It began in Shorter. The location was Shorter, Alabama, in Macon County, an area of Creek Indians located twenty-five miles east of Montgomery and twenty-five miles west of Tuskegee, Alabama.

—OLIVIA CHRISTOPHER (MY PATERNAL GRANDMOTHER)

My grandmother was a proper woman married to my grandfather, Claude, a proper man. When we visited them as kids, I felt delicate and was treated as such, like a porcelain doll visiting a dollhouse. My grandpa was a preacher and leader in the AME Zion Church (as was my father when I was growing up), and they always lived in parsonages, sometimes next door to the churches where they served. The Christopher family may or may not be considered fancy by really fancy people, but to me, there was always an extravagance about them and their homes. Whether in Gary, Indiana (where both my father and Michael Jackson were born), or in Chicago, Illinois (the city they lived in for many years and claimed as home), their large houses always had a good-sized finished attic or basement, and typically a greenhouse or garden patio.

Grandma named the many rooms in her homes by color: the green room, the pink room, and so on. She was always delighted to show off the color-coded decor of each room. Grandma had chores assigned to days too. On Hair Day, she spent the day going through her Black woman hair routine of washing, conditioning, blow-drying, parting, and greasing her scalp, and then drawing sections of her 4C hair up in rollers, and not just the pink sponge ones. I remember her showing me how to roll up our hair with pieces of brown paper bag from the grocery store, and I thought it was such a cool trick. There was also Sewing Day, as she made her own clothes and also took great pride in showing off her smartly selected accessories to match whichever dress pattern she had sewn, sometimes using no pattern at all, only the ones in her head. Shopping Day. Church Day.

She seemed to have Grandpa on a schedule, too, steering him like a well-behaved robot. From my little granddaughter eyes, her whole operation seemed to suit him very well. She and my grandpa had matching cars, which were as dependable as my grandfather was as a father, husband, preacher, and supervisor of other local preachers in the district. They kept their matching, good-gas-mileage cars well maintained as they used them to drive long distances across the country throughout the year, traveling from city to city and state to state for family reunions and general conferences hosted by the denomination. They didn't like to fly, so taking road trips was a normal part of their lives, and we loved when they would come and visit us as they did every year, pulling up to our houses in California and Texas, smelling of Ivory soap, Blue Magic hair grease, Jergens lotion, and the mothballs that Grandma used to preserve all their handmade clothing.

Olivia was the grandma who covered everything in plastic. The couches suffocated in it, as did the chairs and even the carpet that you walked on when you were invited to sit in the formal living room. The floor mats in the matching cars had plastic on them . . . or maybe they were covered in brown paper bags like Grandma's hair when she curled it.

When they were at home, Grandpa could often be found at the kitchen table watching the little TV they kept there, or rather "it would watch him," as Grandma would say, while she cooked all the meals with her Black Southern intuition and know-how.

Grandpa loved her cooking. He loved her, and he made sure everyone knew it.

Olivia was a proper and organized Black woman who had earned her associate's degree in business administration while raising my dad and my aunt.

I was given my middle name after her. Olivia. I even looked like my grandma and would find myself staring into what felt like my own eyes whenever I went through old family albums and saw pictures of young, "foxy" Olivia, as my grandpa used to remark over my shoulder when he'd see old Polaroids of his young bride.

I wanted to be like her, but I often felt far from living up to all the expectations both my parents and grandparents had for me.

Not that I didn't try. For years, I tried to be proper in the way that in sixth grade at the public school in Oak Cliff, Dallas, the Black kids told me I talked funny, earning myself the title of "articulate"—a quality that, as I got older, helped white folx feel comfortable around me. Proper in my grandma Olivia's way, committed to church life and all the ways I was supposed to serve my husband as a godly wife, and "train up a child in the way he should go" so that "when he is old, he will not depart from it" (Proverbs 22:6). Proper as in loving my country and being a good, upstanding Black citizen in order to live the American dream and have all that this democratic nation promised us as Americans.

But holding on to the illusion that being proper would keep me safe would ultimately break my heart in many ways. And I would eventually come to realize that there was more for me than being proper. Because I was more than proper, I was queer.

SIX

Get Therapy

When I found myself at a crossroads of personal, environmental, and social tragedies, I sought out professional help in the form of therapy. The following are excerpts from an article that was published in the *Journal of Psychology and Christianity*, written by two of my former therapists about the intensive therapy retreat I went through in the summer of 2020, which consisted of working with a team of four therapists, four hours a day, over the course of five days. I am the case study client, Olivia.

ARTIFACT

Excerpt from "Honoring the Ori: Mindfulness Meditation at the Intersection of Black Women's Spirituality and Sexualities"

By Natalie Malone and Candice N. Hargons
Department of Educational, School, and Counseling Psychology, University of Kentucky

In the present article, we present a case example for Olivia, a self-identified Black queer woman who experienced spiritual struggle stemming from her Evangelical Christian upbringing and sexualities. We provide insight regarding how we assisted Olivia in honoring her Ori—"the inherent spiritual and sexual identity given to all humans at birth" (Asanti, 2010, p. 29). . . .

Black Feminism and Intersectionality

To conceptualize this case, we used a Black feminist approach called intersectionality (Cole, 2009). Black feminism refers to the collection of values, ideas, and writings put forth by Black scholastic foremothers that outline Black women's historical and sociocultural experiences (Collins, 2002; Crenshaw, 2018). Black feminism also accounts for intersectionality, which describes how multiple forms of oppression intersect and affect Black women (Crenshaw, 2018). Relevant to Olivia's case, Black feminist scholarship examines how slavery and respectability politics amplified by Black Christianity shaped views of Black women's sexualities (Collins, 2002; Day, 2018). Namely, during slavery, Black women created strategies, like "covering up," or modesty, to attempt to thwart (often unsuccessfully) unwanted advances, sexual assault, and rape (Butler, 2007). These strategies later evolved into respectability politics—the adoption of Eurocentric standards to regulate behavior and religious views (Okello, 2020). As a result, Black religious institutions influenced by respectability politics developed more conservative and heteronormative views on sexualities than African indigenous or Eastern religions (Beck, 2003). For example, within theologically conservative Black traditions, people draw on scripture and tradition to limit Black women's sexual expression, agency, and sexual partners to heterosexual and monogamous unions (Day, 2018).

By using Black feminism and intersectionality in therapy, the treatment team aimed to connect with and honor Olivia's "authentic reality" as a woman with three marginalized identities (i.e., Black queer woman) impacted by religion/spirituality (R/S) (Jones & Harris, 2019, p. 251). Accordingly, we integrate elements of Black feminism and intersectionality in the case details and conceptualization.

Case Details: Olivia

Olivia was a forty-one-year-old Black, self-identified queer woman. Black feminism highlights the importance of "naming," which allows clients to call forth their most salient identities. For Olivia, her intersectional identities as a Black queer woman and activist were important. As an anti-Black racism and social justice educator, Olivia demonstrated an internalization-commitment Black racial identity. Characteristics of this racial identity included valuing and having a positive orientation towards her Blackness and a commitment to social activism (Carter, 1991). Olivia's presenting concerns included past wounds from religion and society that affected her sexualities. While she was no longer affiliated with Evangelical Christianity, she maintained spiritual practices, including meditation, hiking, African tarot reading, and manifestation using divine feminine power (Afua, 2001). When she entered therapy, she described herself as being in a state of sexual exploration, including a desire to embrace her attraction to any gender unapologetically and engage her curiosities.

Background Information

Olivia's early socialization was heavily influenced by her educated, lower-middle-class background and Evangelical Christian upbringing in a predominantly Black church. Olivia's father was a well-known conservative Christian leader, which placed Olivia's family at the forefront of their religious community. Olivia received strong messages related to Black women's race and sexualities. For example, her father always emphasized that her family was conservative Christian before Black, which meant supporting women's traditional gender roles and anti-gay messages and causes.

During early adulthood, Olivia entered her first marriage, a Black heterosexual union, but continued to experience same-gender attraction and struggled to navigate her desires. She described experiencing sexual dreams with other women and waking up in terror next to her husband. She called upon women of the church to pray over her and dismiss the negative spirits attacking her. Amid these experiences, her marriage began to suffer for reasons other than sexuality and ended in divorce. As Olivia embarked on a new self-journey, she began to explore her sexualities, came out as

queer at the age of thirty, and left organized religion. Her sexual exploration evolved as she dated and initiated sexual relationships more often with women. Olivia entered her second marriage to a Black woman she described as her soul mate. However, despite their connection, Olivia found herself in a mothering role based on the significant age difference between her and her partner. At the time of treatment, Olivia and her wife experienced interpersonal dysfunction and effectively separated, which left Olivia in need of social support.

Conceptualization

Olivia's case relied on a Black Feminist and intersectional approach to therapy that conceptualized her presenting concern as the result of the multiplicative oppressions she experienced as a queer Black woman unaffiliated with Christianity (Jones, 2015). Her symptoms included sadness, stress, social isolation, anxiety, and panic. These symptoms were the result of years of gendered racism and heterosexism experienced in her daily life, from family members, and from the Christian community. The values she inherited as a Black Christian woman emerged from respectability politics, such as holiness practices, idolized cisgender heterosexual marriage, monogamy, and patriarchal submission (Moultrie, 2018). Thus, her same-gender attraction and sexually progressive values were incongruent with the religious teachings she received. This incongruity resulted in spiritual struggle, causing Olivia to feel stress, pain, and psychological and existential distress (Exline et al., 2014; Pargament & Exline, 2020).

Treatment Process

Healing Circle

Olivia intentionally sought out a Black woman therapist (the second author) who then created a healing circle for Olivia with three additional Black women clinicians. Stemming from the African ring shout tradition among enslaved African women, collective healing circles in Black feminist therapy offer Black women "emotional and physical release" within a community of gendered racially similar peers (Richardson, 2018, p. 285). Naming the clinician's social location in relation to clients is another critical element of Black feminist therapy (Asanti, 2010). The treatment team consisted of four Black, college-educated, able-bodied, ciswomen clinicians. . . .

Culturally Adapted Mindfulness with Olivia

Aligning MBIs [mindfulness-based interventions] with the client's spiritual practice is one way to make mindfulness more applicable to Black women

(Biggers et al., 2020). Each day of Olivia's intensive retreat began with a mindfulness meditation intervention and body scan. During her meditation, we emphasized components of mindfulness that overlapped with her African indigenous spiritual beliefs. For example, chanting and *mantras* are mindful practices associated with the mind-body connection—a core piece of Buddhist and African spiritualties. Similar to Buddhist *mantras* or meditative chants (e.g., *Om Mani Padme Hum*), chants ground the chanter within the body and focus their attention (Pereira, 2016), which may lead to a "stillness" with self or God (Biggers et al., 2020). Olivia received an invitation to use meditative chants during her MBI as a way to "be still" with herself and spirit.

A second adaptation we made to Olivia's MBI was the addition of an ancestral healing ritual. Rituals are a common healing technique in the African diaspora that facilitate a connection to ancestral spirits (Bojuwoye, 2005). True to the value of communalism in African culture (Etta et al., 2016), rituals are often successful when conducted in community with others (Somé, 2000). To begin the ancestral healing ritual, the first author invited Olivia to imagine her ancestors. Ancestors may include family or loved ones who transitioned to heaven or other spiritual planes (Dionne, 2020). After envisioning her ancestors, the first author offered a prayer that invited Olivia's ancestors to share spiritual downloads, or messages, with her that she then vocalized to Olivia. Olivia's ancestors offered her love, acceptance, and divine blessing. These messages were particularly important to Olivia as a queer woman, because they upheld the alternative perspective of some African indigenous belief systems that recognize Black LGBTQIA+ people as divinely blessed (Asanti, 2010, p. 25).

To promote the acceptance and non-judgmental awareness of her sexualities, we added sexual mindfulness activities. Olivia completed breathing exercises, chakra healing, tantric masturbation rituals, and fantasy envisioning (Black Girl Bliss, 2018; Gethin, 2011; Sayin, 2017). These activities helped transform her body into a medium for enlightenment, divinity, and fulfillment by aligning her with her sacral and heart chakras (Bullis, 1998). Additionally, these activities helped Olivia observe her thoughts and feelings about her sexualities while engaging in self-pleasure in non-judgmental and non-self-critical ways.

By the end of the retreat, Olivia was able to relax, identify her emotions, cultivate self-compassion, and embrace loving-kindness. Olivia mindfully crafted fantasy around her sexualities and queerness. She acknowledged the shame, stigma, and sense of rejection she felt in her past related to her sexual desires. In line with her spirit, Olivia asserted that at this point in her life, she could depart from her early socialization in sexualities and replace it with something new. She manifested and embarked on her new sexual agreement with herself—an agreement solidified through mindfulness: "In the future, my sexuality will be a tremendously big, happy, peaceful, joyful, playful, creative part of my life." Mindfulness led to this new sexual agreement by facilitating increased compassion, acceptance, and a deeper understanding of self (Kirmayer, 2015). To date, Olivia continues participating in and reflecting on the activities after the retreat.

SEVEN

Black Suffering

Black people comprise 13 percent of the US population but roughly 30 percent of the arrested, 35 percent of the imprisoned, 42 percent of those on death row, and 56 percent of those serving life sentences.

The United States incarcerates more humans than any other country on the planet, a disproportionate number of them Black. The Black community is suffering, and as long as our suffering goes unresolved, we are not free. There will always be the threat of Black death and the effects of trauma among an entire group of people who are stuck there because we have not been allowed the space and time, or the truth and reconciliation, that would usher in our collective ability to grieve and to heal.

How long would we sing these Black funeral songs before we burned shit down?

The answer to that question would come in the summer of 2020, as the world watched the outpouring of Black American protest chants and rallies at courthouses and police stations across the landscape, vigils in neighborhoods, requests for money to pay attorneys' fees and cover burial and memorial services for poor Black families left behind. BLACK LIVES MATTER. The entire planet felt these words, much as the world felt the ringing of the words of Dr. King during the March on Washington, when he proclaimed hopefully, "Free at last, free at last, thank God Almighty, we are free at last." Sadly, in 2020, as more people of

all races and nations declared that Black Lives Mattered, we simultaneously acknowledged that we are not fucking free at last. Every time we say Black Lives
Matter, it is an attempt to convince and persuade a criminally guilty US government that our Black lives are worthy.

EIGHT

False Allyship

If you have come here to help me, you're wasting your time. If you have come because your liberation is bound up with mine, then let us work together.

—LILLA WATSON

J ust a week before Nate's execution, five of the 2020 Democratic presidential candidates gathered in Selma, Alabama, to commemorate the fifty-fifth anniversary of Bloody Sunday and the Voting Rights Act. The candidates went to great lengths to explain how much they cared about Black lives, but the following week when it came time to intervene on behalf of a Black man facing the death penalty for NOT killing someone, none of the candidates did anything to save Nate's life. False allyship was the badge that the Democratic presidential candidates gave themselves and wore arrogantly next to their USA flag pins on their red, white, or blue lapels as they walked across the Edmund Pettus Bridge and smiled for the cameras. For many white Americans, there is too much benefit of the doubt lying around, being distributed on Main Street, USA, whereas no such benefits were granted to the indigenous people on whom Plymouth Rock landed.

The history books in public schools, written, approved, and distributed by white authors and white school boards, have consistently told the story of America in a way that fails to hold the nation responsible for its crimes against humanity and its ongoing legacy of genocide, slavery, and racial exploitation. So non-Black knowledge of the construct of race and how it operates is grossly limited and incomplete. Stories told by white teachers following white lesson plans in schools all over the nation have kept the Black story carefully restricted and confined. White people committed to whiteness and white supremacy have wrongly assumed they know about us and our history and falsely imply that our lives were just enough like theirs for them not to pay attention to the grave injustices our community experiences at the hands of the present-day government. Hence, "All Lives Matter."

The reality of false allyship among white folx who were all emotional and ready to jump on the activism bandwagon after Ahmaud Arbery and George Floyd were killed is why Black folx were suspicious and disillusioned by the sudden show of white support during the racial uprisings of the summer of 2020. Many Black leaders, Black women in particular, knew that the white urgency of the summer of 2020 was a result of false and performative allyship. A lot of white folx were having emotional reactions to the racial moment instead of a clear, grounded, embodied commitment to a racial and radical movement to fight and dismantle white supremacy.

Though BLM had started back in 2013, the summer of 2020 was when white America tried picking up the BLM mantle as a great display of solidarity fanfare and ally theatrics. Momentarily. And as with everything else that whiteness touches, the social stock and racial capital of wokeness skyrocketed and corporations began the low vibrating hum of BLM. All of a white sudden, BLM was brought to us by corporate sponsors. It was the trending phrase of that summer. White mics were passed to Black mouths, though with much restriction and gatekeeping, of course. White tables pulled up Black chairs in much the same way that kiddie chairs were pulled up to the "adults' table" during family gatherings and holidays. All things Black became a spectacle of white fawning. White gasps. Black eye rolls. White questions. Black answers. White confusion. Black annoyance. White apathy. Black grief.

Well, we were trying to grieve. Everybody Black. Rooting for each other to keep our heads up like Tupac told us, while white folx said bless our hearts. We were trying to hold space for ourselves and one another, but white hysteria kept interrupting, blaring BLM through defund the police bullhorns.

We went from Ahmaud Arbery to Nate Woods to Breonna Taylor to George Floyd. From Georgia to Alabama to Kentucky to Minnesota. From stay-at-home moms in Silicon Valley to Sweet Not-Staying-Home Alabama dads. It was a whole-ass moment for those of us who had already been doing antiracism facilitation and education.

Suddenly, a white audience appeared in every one of our once virtually empty virtual seats. Newly self-appointed and self-identified white allies drooled for more; they were collecting Black influencers from the corners of Facebook to the edges of Instagram. Black antiracism followings and patrons surged, and in response, all antiracism content creators went beyond work into overtime. This moment was our time—Black supply to their white demand.

Virtual workshops and black tiles exploded all over Instagram like Fourth of July fireworks, overdue justice reminiscent of the late arrival of the news of emancipation on June 19, 1865, in Galveston, Texas. We Black folx were tired, and also, Black antiracism educators were somewhat energized. White people "ran for Maud," not realizing that by the time we got to marching for George, they would soon run out of fucks to give. Black folx knew this co-opted BLM moment would not last. I knew that for me to step away from my antiracism work at this particular moment of white attention was necessary . . . I was starting to hate white people.

I have been so afraid to say that, to write that, but that is what was brewing below the surface of my righteous Black rage. I was struggling to cope with all the Black death of the times and got to a place where I could no longer help myself, so I could no longer help the whites. The work of antiracism would still be there waiting for me when I came back to it. Racism wasn't going anywhere. I couldn't save us. I had to try to save myself.

White people, keep your false allyship. Give me, give us, your radicalized activism.

NINE

One Nation under Black Trauma

And as of today, if I am asked abroad if I am a free citizen of the United States of America, I must only say what is true: No.

—LORRAINE HANSBERRY

Emmett Till's mother made the heart-wrenching choice to have her disfigured son's casket left open and allow the publication of graphic pictures of what white supremacy had done. Her decision was about her as a mother, wanting to show the global community what it meant, and what it looked like, for a Black mother to grieve her murdered Black son. If anyone was going to attempt to understand the threat of Black death and collective Black suffering and grief, they needed to see her precious son, dead and disfigured.

As she famously said, "I want the world to see what they did to my son."

The trauma that spread through the Black community upon the sight and knowledge of the horrors that took place against Emmett Till and Trayvon Martin sparked movements in both the 1950s and the 2010s. And despite full knowledge of the identities of their white killers, much as in the case of Breonna Taylor's murder, no one was ever held accountable for the murders of Emmett Till or Trayvon Martin.

For the hanged and beaten.
For the shot, drowned, and burned.
For the tortured, tormented, and terrorized.
For those abandoned by the rule of law.

We will remember.

With hope because hopelessness is the enemy of justice.
With courage because peace requires bravery.
With persistence because justice is a constant struggle.
With faith because we shall overcome.

—*The National Memorial for Peace and Justice*
Montgomery, Alabama

I submit that our Black grief is our reminder that we are not free. Our Black grief is our reminder that we must continue to fight and strive for, imagine and create ways to get free so that we no longer have to sing our Black sorrow songs. Our Black grief is our wake-up call that we have been given these blessed, Black bodies, and it is up to us to love and support each other, and to grieve and heal ourselves, on personal levels as well as collectively, as we find ways to get free and walk each other home.

If Black grief can move white folx to want to fight for change, then so be it. But Black grief is not on display so white folx can give a fuck. White allies and white friends can care about our Black grief and our Black suffering and our Black trauma, but white validation is unnecessary as it relates to Black grief. Black grief is sacred and belongs to Black people. Our grief is not for white folx to use as motivational material and has nothing to do with whiteness. We deserve, and it is time that we demand, to grieve in peace.

* * *

ARTIFACT

Emmett Till Antilynching Act

In consideration of the Black suffering and Black trauma that Black Americans have endured and experienced in this nation, I invite you to carefully read the words of the bill that was introduced to the House of Representatives, by Representative Bobby Rush of Illinois on January 24, 2021, to specify lynching as a hate crime act. The Emmett Till Antilynching Act (H.R. 55) was finally signed into law on March 29, 2022.

H.R. 55

IN THE HOUSE OF REPRESENTATIVES
January 4, 2021
Mr. Rush introduced the following bill;
which was referred to the Committee on the Judiciary

A BILL

To amend section 249 of title 18, United States Code, to specify lynching as a hate crime act.

Be it enacted by the Senate and House of Representatives of the United States of America in Congress assembled,

SECTION 1. SHORT TITLE.

This Act may be cited as the "Emmett Till Antilynching Act".

SEC. 2. FINDINGS.

Congress finds the following:

(1) In the 20th century lynching occurred mostly in southern States by White southerners against Black southerners.

(2) In 1892, the Tuskegee Institute began to record statistics of lynchings and reported that 4,742 reported lynchings had taken place by 1968, of which 3,445 of the victims were Black.

(3) Most of the lynchings that occurred in the South were mass moblike lynchings.

(4) Mass moblike lynchings were barbaric by nature characterized by members of the mob, mostly White southerners, shooting, burning, and mutilating the victim's body, alive.

(5) In "Anatomy of a Lynching: The Killing of Claude Neal", community papers readily advertised mob lynchings, as evidenced by a Florida local paper headline: "Florida to Burn Negro at Stake: Sex Criminal Seized from Brewton Jail, Will be Mutilated, Set Afire in Extra-Legal Vengeance for Deed."

(6) Civil rights groups documented and presented Congress evidence of vigilante moblike lynchings.

(7) Evidence by NAACP investigator Howard Kester documented the extreme brutality of these lynchings. An excerpt from "Anatomy of a Lynching" further illustrates this point: "After taking the nigger to the woods about four miles from Greenwood, they cut off his penis. He was made to eat it. Then they cut off his testicles and made him eat them and say he liked it."

(8) Many civil rights groups, notably the Anti-Lynching Crusaders, also known as the ALC, operating under the umbrella of the NAACP, made numerous requests to Congress to make lynching a Federal crime.

(9) Congressman George Henry White, an African American, introduced the first Federal antilynching bill and subsequently nearly 200 anti-lynching bills were introduced in the Congress during the first half of the 20th century.

(10) Between 1890 and 1952, seven Presidents petitioned Congress to end lynching.

(11) Between 1920 and 1940, the House of Representatives passed three strong anti-lynching measures, of which Congress came closest to enacting anti-lynching legislation sponsored by Congressman Leonidas C. Dyer in 1922.

(12) On all three occasions, opponents of anti-lynching legislation, argued States' rights and used the filibuster, or the threat of it, to block the Senate from voting on the measures.

(13) The enactment of the Civil Rights Act of 1968 was the closest Congress ever came in the post-Reconstruction era to enacting anti-lynching legislation.

(14) In 2005, the Senate passed a resolution, sponsored by Senators Mary Landrieu and George Allen, apologizing for the Senate's failure to enact anti-lynching legislation as a Federal crime, with Senator Landrieu saying, "There may be no other injustice in American history for which the Senate so uniquely bears responsibility."

(15) To heal past and present racial injustice, Congress must make lynching a Federal crime so our Nation can begin reconciliation.

SEC. 3. SPECIFYING LYNCHING AS A HATE CRIME ACT.

Section 249(a) of title 18, United States Code, is amended--

(1) by redesignating paragraph (4) as paragraph (5); and

(2) by inserting after paragraph (3) the following:

"(4) OFFENSES INVOLVING LYNCHING.—Whoever, whether or not acting under color of law, willfully, acting as part of any collection of people, assembled for the purpose and with the intention of committing an act of violence upon any person, causes death to any person, shall be imprisoned for any term of years or for life, fined under this title, or both."

TEN

A Black American
Horror Story from Texas

In September 2018, Botham Jean, a twenty-six-year-old Black man and native of Saint Lucia, who resided in Dallas, Texas, was eating ice cream and watching TV when Dallas police officer Amber Guyger entered his apartment and fatally shot him. Guyger later told police she mistook him for a burglar and his apartment for her own. She was charged with his murder that October.

In the summer of 2019, my wife, Dawn, and I were living in a suburb of Dallas, and I was volunteering for a local group of formerly incarcerated activists and organizers who were working toward ending money bail and mass incarceration in Dallas. One afternoon in September, we were talking about the upcoming local murder trial for Amber Guyger, and I decided to go.

Having been so deeply devastated by police killings of Black people, I wanted to attend the proceedings to understand what took place between the prosecution and the defense, the jury and the judge, what we heard in the media as compared to what actually happened inside the courtroom.

I had recently retired from my fitness career in order to do my antiracism and racial justice work full-time, and so I was able to prioritize being present for the murder trial. For three days, I arrived at the Dallas courthouse early to ensure that I would get one of the few seats that were open and available to the public. As I sat inside Judge Tammy Kemp's courtroom, next to the mothers of both Botham Jean and Amber Guyger, I listened intently and took copious notes. At the conclusion of each day, I would go live on Facebook to talk about what had taken place during the trial throughout the day.

I listened to hours of testimony and watched hours of footage from body cams, including Amber Guyger's body cam, recorded after she drew and fired her gun and then left Botham Jean lying in his own blood, fighting for his life, while she called 911 but made no attempts to administer CPR or any other technique that could have saved his life. I bore witness to so many details, from the eyewitness accounts of the first responding officers on the scene, to the corruption of the Dallas Police Association, which intervened at the crime scene immediately following the shooting in an attempt to protect Amber Guyger; from the investigation by the Texas Rangers, to evidence that the judge wouldn't allow the jurors to hear.

I will never forget watching Joshua Brown, another young Black man and one of Bo's neighbors, who entered the courtroom and walked right past me wearing a T-shirt and shorts, looking disheveled and disoriented, taking the stand and telling us how he remembered hearing Bo singing in his apartment. As Joshua told the story, he broke down in tears. And when Joshua Brown was shot and killed just ten days after he testified, I attended a local candlelight vigil in his honor. I believe, along with many Black activists in Dallas, that his testimony in the Amber Guyger trial exposed him to danger and put his life at risk.

I hugged Bo's father. I fixed Amber's mother's tag on the back of her blouse as I sat behind her one day. In that small space, where we all held the tension and our grief, for different reasons and for different people, we were connected to one another with a shared anxiety and sense of dread, along with the weight of the racial and historical implications and significance of what this trial represented. Two families, one white and one Black. One dead Black man. One alive white woman on trial for taking his life. Two perspectives, one of accusation, the other of "an honest mistake."

This murder trial was as American as it gets. I sat there between the two families, and the two races, taking it all in. I had a front-row seat to another Black American Horror Story, this one taking place in real time. And despite how the trials of police officers who publicly execute Black victims usually go, that multiracial jury delivered a murder verdict to that Black woman judge, who was slammed by the media and public opinion for hugging Amber Guyger and giving her a Bible after finding her guilty of murder.

During the sentencing phase, Bo's brother famously read a victim impact statement in which he granted forgiveness to Amber Guyger. The guilty verdict was felt by the Black community across the nation, not just for Bo but because there was hope that this would set a precedent and more police officers would be held accountable for taking Black lives.

Two families wept that day, though for different reasons.

We are one nation living under Black trauma, and we had no way of knowing how the events that took place during that murder trial and the overdue murder conviction that it delivered would affect us Black folx.

What was this strange, grief-laced relief? Surely, we were not free yet.

ELEVEN

Find Stillness Every Day through Breath

Between stimulus and response there is a space. In that space is our power to choose our response. In our response lies our growth and our freedom.

—VIKTOR FRANKL

Eric Garner was a Black man killed by the NYPD in July 2014. While being pinned to the sidewalk in a chokehold, he repeated the words "I can't breathe" eleven times. They still suffocated him to death. His last words identify one of the very important tools that we must use to get free: our breath. When we no longer breathe, there is no life. When we breathe, we live.

In a society that does not value and has great disregard for our Black humanity, the restriction of our breath is used as a weapon of oppression. However, this also means that our breath is a key to our liberation and to life.

It is in our breath, our "prana," our life force, that we notice sensation. It is the breath that connects us to our ability to feel and to move. If we reclaim our breath, if we own our breath, if we commit to preserving our precious breath in the ways we wish we could have preserved and protected Eric's breath, we will gather for ourselves a powerful liberatory practice.

As Black people, we can no longer afford not to breathe with great purpose, intention, and love. In many Black traditions, we often declare that to wake up each morning to see a new day is a blessing, a gift. And it is in that same spirit that we must rise, honor, revere, and reclaim our breath. This is true for all of us, all of humanity.

In our breath, we will find both the prayer offered and the prayer answered.

In stillness, we find our breath. Our opportunity for healing invites us to be with it, to sit with it. After you become accustomed to noticing your own breath, observing your heart beating, see what else arises. You will begin to notice things about yourself and many other alive things with a deeper appreciation and gratitude. In stillness and breath, you will gain a greater awareness of all that is holy in your Black being and all living beings and creatures. The soft wind will start to feel like the brush of a gentle kiss. And this will feel good to you (this is pleasure). Your senses will be heightened, and you will start to seek out opportunities to be still and breathe because you will notice that there is freedom in the stillness, freedom in the space between all the movement. Embody your breath, embody your life.

As activists, we must find that blessed space between the moments of trauma and grief and work and bills and family and obligation, and freedom. Our breath can begin to teach us just how possible freedom truly is.

Find a method that works for you and set aside time every day to learn and cultivate a breathing/mindfulness practice. Find a meditation guide or a class or a mindfulness coach. Download a meditation app (see the Liberate app for and by queer BIPOC mindfulness practitioners). It is imperative that you learn how using your breath with intention can shift how your body feels and how it functions and enable you to start to process the traumas that we are exposed to on a daily basis and connect to your ability to heal. When you start to breathe, you start to feel. When you start to feel, you start to notice. When you start to notice, a lot will arise. You may get angry and/or sad. But you will also come alive in a way that you become connected to your deepest self, your inner voice, and the messages and blessings that the ancestors have been sending you from the moment you arrived on this planet.

As babies arriving through the portal of our mothers' wombs, we knew this; we came here remembering. But as we grew older, we stopped exploring the world through play and our senses. We switched into a breathless mode of operating because white supremacy, capitalism, and the patriarchy function better when we don't feel. Our hearts and lungs hardened and our breath became short and restricted because we could not hold both the unaddressed grief and the oppression and function in a society built to keep our bodies weary and broken and short of breath. So in order to change the dynamic in the relationship between who we are as Black humans and what we can choose to do, we must restore the connection to our breath. Our spirit will meet us there. If you have a higher power, your breath, like the womb we all come through at birth, is a portal to a deeper relationship with that life-sustaining source. We access it through the exact same channel that the police officers cut off when they killed Eric Garner: by utilizing our breath.

TWELVE

Reaching the (Housing) Limit of Racialized Trauma

As new nomads, my wife and I were living in the Atlanta area when COVID-19 hit. But in April, Governor Brian Kemp put a ban on temporary housing, and I learned that in the United States in 2020, my housing was insecure, uncertain, and dependent on the state. This wasn't something that I had anticipated when we left our rental house in Little Elm, Texas, back in January, but it was an important thing to learn as we began our nomadic journey. Instead of closing beaches, the state came in and decided to put transient people and folx with temporary housing needs, like us, at risk.

We were not leisure travelers; we were nomads. We had made an intentional decision to move from place to place and eventually exit the country and become expats because we no longer felt safe or free in our own country. It was no sweet land of liberty for queer Black women like us. We were looking for a better life. The experiment was to find out if there was a country on the planet where we could feel safe in our skin. This was as much the guiding question for us as "Are we free yet?"

By definition, I am effectively "homeless," though I don't typically use that word because I have chosen this lifestyle, and that's where my own privilege lies. I made the conscious decision to stop renting a house or apartment, to not buy a home, to stop paying all household bills in hopes of finding some sense of financial, political, and social freedom that seemed to elude me as a queer Black woman who was a citizen of the US by and since birth. I chose to become location-independent in an attempt to take care of myself as much as possible outside of the structures and systems of the US government, which is clearly not concerned with protecting or providing for my queer Black life. In drastically reducing my expenses and making plans to leave the country to become an expat, I was attempting to create a pathway for myself that felt free.

Because of the ban, we left Georgia and went to Tennessee. There was no rhyme or reason in choosing Tennessee. We got on Airbnb's website, looked at the map, and landed where we found a beautiful home in the mountains in a town called Kingsport. From this designer home, standing on the balcony, we could see the mountains in four different states.

On the Saturday before Mother's Day, Dawn went out into the mountains to hike, and I decided to stay back and have some alone time. After taking a shower, and still in a towel, I sat on the couch and opened my Liberate app to listen to a meditation led by Dr. Candice Hargons, the director of the Center for Healing Racial Trauma in Kentucky. She was talking about racial stress and trauma and how it stays in the body and the ways that Black folx react when we have experienced a racial stressor such as all the killings of Black folx by cops and the graphic videos of our deaths going viral.

While I was listening to her, I heard someone enter the keypad code to open the front door. I assumed that it was Dawn returning from her hike. When the door opened, I wasn't paying much attention, but after several seconds went by, I heard faint voices, but not her voice. Then the door closed. I got up and went to the door and out of habit locked it as I looked through the peephole. I didn't see her or our car. I unlocked the door and opened it, and no one was there.

After I made a few attempts to call her and didn't get through, she finally picked up.

"Are you here?"

"No, I'm hiking."

I told her someone had just opened the front door of our condo and then quickly left. She raced back home to me. I was freaking out. My mind was back in Dallas, at the courthouse, in the murder trial. I was stunned and having flashbacks.

Dawn returned, yelling at our Airbnb host over the phone, while I sat on the couch, shaking, still wearing only a towel, my mind reviewing the part of the murder trial that was focused on the way Amber Guyger had entered Bo's apartment, how she had been able to gain entrance into an apartment that wasn't hers. The prosecutors spent a lot of time focusing on the function of the door and exactly how it worked. They brought in door experts. They analyzed how quickly she entered the wrong apartment, assumed it was her own, saw Botham Jean sitting on his couch with a bowl of ice cream in his hands after having his wisdom teeth removed a few days earlier. As he started to stand up upon hearing someone enter his apartment, she drew her gun, she aimed, she fired, she killed him.

It all happened in a matter of seconds.

I'm in Pigeon Forge.

I'm in a courtroom in Dallas.

I'm in Bo's apartment.

I'm in a borrowed condo.

I need a door expert.

I need a flashback expert.

This is how and when I met Dr. Candice. Having listened to her talk just moments earlier about the trauma that Black people experience due to racial triggers and responses, I Googled her name and found her Facebook page and website.

I sent her a message, and surprisingly, she responded quickly. That night, we had an emergency session, our first of many calls that would turn into weekly therapy sessions.

JOURNAL PROMPT

Consider and write about how safe you feel at home in your bed, in your home, in your neighborhood. Then, consider what safety looked like for Breonna Taylor.

ARTIFACT

"Healing Racial Trauma with Dr. Candice Nicole Hargons"

Speaking of Racism Podcast
Excerpt from November 18, 2020

Tina: So, can you explain a little bit more about what Black folx likely are feeling and experiencing during this time when there is this onslaught of not only anti-Black violence and terror and killings, but how accessible it is for us to see on recording and on videos. Can you speak to that a little bit?

Dr. Candice Nicole Hargons: Yeah. So racial trauma is like a pathway. It starts with race-based stress reactions, which most people get. Those are the immediate, unintentional, unconscious reactions you get when you're exposed to a racist stimulus or a racist stressor. And that could be a systemic racist stress, or a personally mediated one, even sometimes internalized pieces. So these videos, these audios, these social media sharing of all of these instances of racism are racist stressors. And most of us appraise them as stressful. And then our bodies and our emotions and our thoughts start reacting.

So, in our research, we talk about that as a vicarious racial stimulus or racist stimulus. It does not even have to happen to you. It can be happening to someone that looks like you, and you still get a sense for it. And there are

three levels of that reaction. So you have somatic reactions. You might find yourself having a harder time breathing, your hands might be shaking, your body might be shaking, you might start crying, you might feel, like, tension in your stomach, a lot of people carry that in their shoulders, in their neck, their jawline, like you feel yourself getting tight, shaky, and physically unsettled. That's a somatic reaction. For our research, we call that "letting out," when you have a reaction to racism that you don't hold in but you let out, your body lets it out whether or not you want it to.

And then there's another level where it's an emotional reaction. And we call this "sitting with," because for most Black people, you're socialized to not express affect, because it could be dangerous. But for some people, you feel and are able to identify anger and rage or sadness or heartbreak, any spectrum of emotions, sometimes even numbness and apathy when it's just worn you out. So that's another typical reaction.

And then additionally, we have what we call a "rising above" reaction. But it's a cognitive reaction. It's a series of thought patterns, where you start to explain it away, so that you don't have to confront the physical and emotional sadness or consequences of that. You might justify, even depending on how you were raised, why something racist happened in the way it happened.

But you also might, if you're really a little bit further along in your critical consciousness, you might start to intellectualize it. So you know it's wrong, but you're dismantling every level of that racist experience in arguments. So it's one that you might see a person using if someone says something microaggressive, and then they give them a litany of, like, reasons why that's untrue, and facts and stats, like that's a rising above reaction.

For many people, the rising above is because you've been socialized not to have access to feelings and sensations anymore. And so it's the only way you can grapple with what's happening when you're experiencing a racist encounter. For some of us, though, it's because we don't want to feel anymore, we're tired of feeling. And we feel like to broker our other privileges, maybe our linguistic privilege or intellectual privilege or even financial privilege, educational privilege, can do enough for that moment to where you don't feel brought low by the racist encounter.

Tina: Can you tell me what you would suggest and recommend for Black folx today, in particular those living in the US: How can we protect ourselves?

How can we heal ourselves? What are some tips and maybe strategies that you can recommend for us to care for ourselves, especially at this time?

Dr. Candice: Yeah. I want to name that I don't believe that safety and protection are real things. And I know that's unfortunate, but I have to be in that awareness . . .

Tina: Could you repeat that for me?

Dr. Candice: I don't believe safety and protection are real things.

Tina: Okay.

Dr. Candice: And I know that is an unfortunate way to frame it. But I think to put the reality of that out there helps us divorce from respectability politics. Because a lot of people believe that if I just speak in a certain way, or if I dress in a certain way, or if I act in a certain way, my behavior can dictate whether or not I am at risk of violence. And you don't have any control over how people respond to you. And so, just knowing that we don't have control over other people's, like, violence and response and reaction to their own racism is liberating.

That means that it gives you room to do the things that are healing and facilitate your wellness, like just be, figure out who you are divested from all of these things that whiteness says you should be. That is the therapy. That is the free-99 version of it, figuring out who you want to be, how you want to show up in the world, and recognizing that there isn't any safety provided by assimilating.

Now, there's proximity to resources, so I don't want to deny that. If you assimilate, you can gain proximity to certain resources. But is it worth it? Because does the resource facilitate your wellness, or does it just allow you to move up in a hierarchy that shouldn't exist?

Tina: What do you call—that, what you just described, I understand to be internalized racism and unpacking our own internalized oppression and white supremacy. Is that a term that you would also subscribe to? Or how—could you speak to that a little bit more?

Dr. Candice: Absolutely. I think there's the internalized racism component of it, but I understand it, and I can empathize with it as born out of survival, what you think you have to do to survive. So I've never—for anyone along the spectrum of internalized racism, I never say it in judgment, or like, "You're a terrible Black person, because you have internalized racism or because you endorse certain respectability politics." I get

why, I understand why and how many generations of socialization you're contending with when you make those choices.

But it is, at the end of the day, an endorsement of "This is what I have to do and so I'm going to do it." And also, "I'm going to teach other people to do it, because I think it will help them live," or "I think it will help them get the resources that we want, or that we should have already had access to anyway." So it creates this pathway through scarcity to abundance that shouldn't exist. It should just be that we're living abundantly, that we recognize that sharing is a part of interdependence.

And so, operating just in interdependence, operating in a sense of abundance, operating in courage, where you choose resistance, you recognize what things you're willing to risk, and what fears come up for you. Right, just understandable fears, given the violence of racism, but then you understand and set for yourself, "This is what I'm willing to go forward with, though. This is how I'm willing to push against that." All of those are really wellness-facilitating ways of being.

And then at the core of it, you had to take care of your body and your mind too. The therapy is essential, because you're talking about decades, for most of us, of unpacking, living in, or swimming in the water of racism. And the physical activity is essential. This is what I'm grappling with for myself now and reclaiming. So I do a lot of meditation work, but that's still mind-body, but more mind, like I'm sitting, I'm breathing, I'm doing my breath work. Now I need physical activity.

And so I'm just taking all of the excuses off the table for myself and like, "I need to walk, I need to move, I need to dance, I need to get some physical activity because otherwise I can't do this sustainably." And so that's a part of our wellness as Black people. We deserve that.

THIRTEEN

Heartbreak Is a Gray Grief
for Activists

Two days after someone entered the keypad code and opened the door of our Airbnb, Dawn announced that she wanted to separate. My heart and brain froze. Shock and surprise were immediately replaced with irritation. What kind of fucking announcement is this? What is the problem? I wasn't really paying attention to the words she was saying. I remember she referenced that she had a DMT trip the previous month, and that it was revealed to her that she wasn't supposed to be with me. She said other words in a language that I forgot. The letters and syllables went past me, never landing anywhere near my ears or my comprehension. She would later tell me that she had said that we should treat this separation as permanent as possible. But my frozen heart/brain didn't hear that part either.

Something about needing a break, needing to go find herself.

As I was seven years her elder, I unintentionally took on a management role between us, which was easy to do as I was the one with three kids. By the end of that day, my frozen brain had thawed to manager brain because that is what saves me when I get into my survival instinct of fight. My emotions typically shut down so my logical brain can come in and assess the situation and start doing damage control.

There was a lot going on in what now felt like this tiny heart space inside my chest. Perhaps in my most intense times of fear and pain, my heart shrinks back to the size it was when I was seven years old, and in my mind, I go to a place where I had the best mom who seemed to be able to fix everything.

My mother was a very beautiful Black woman with very light skin, from New Orleans, Louisiana. She was so "high yellow," as we say in the Black community, that I remember one of her kindergarten students asking her why she had a brown daughter, pointing at a very brown me. The shades of grief and skin blur here, as do the lines in the trauma bond sand: my mom couldn't fix this for me. Just as Bo's mom and Amber's mom couldn't fix it for them. And now, how would I fix this?

My mom's yellow skin, and her mom's . . . descended directly from the New Orleans Voodoo queen herself, Marie Laveau.

Bo's mom's dark brown skin, bronzed by the sun in Saint Lucia, where she birthed and raised her Black-skinned son.

Amber's mom's white skin that she passed down to her white daughter . . . did she raise Amber to manage and fix bad situations with her tears?

Emmett's mother's light-skinned Black woman face cried tears that couldn't fix this for her son.

My not-dark-skinned, not-light-skinned, queer Black woman body did not have the headspace to understand how white fingers entered codes unlocking Black doors, nor did I have the heartspace to understand why my wife was leaving me.

A few days later, she was gone.

A POEM ON SEPARATION AND SURVIVING

While I was going through a
   separation from my spouse
Our country was going through a
   separation too
We were getting separated from the
   notion of ourselves
We were as true as we thought we
   could be
We could not imagine a truth that
   existed where we would see ourselves

unfavorably on a national scale, and
   that vision would seep into each and
   every one of our homes
When my wife told me she was leaving
It took me back to the moment on the
   very first day that we heard the
   pandemic song that wouldn't end
The first announcement that things
   were shutting down due to
   COVID-19

That time when everyone raced to the
grocery store to get all the
essentials, not what they needed,
no, beyond that . . .
Our time was up.
My wife walking out the door was my
time being up
With her and the way we had lived our
lives for the past seven and a half
years.
Nationally our time was up
On going to public places without fear
of catching or giving sickness and
death to our stranger neighbor.
We fell into a panic, then resignation,
And panic looked different for
different folx.
Panic for me when my wife left me
alone and homeless in Pigeon
Forge, Tennessee, looked like
irritation, a frozen steel box closing
around first my stomach, then my
chest, then my throat.
Panic for Americans looked like fear of
not having anything to wipe our
butts with when we took a shit.
We raced to do something,
To try and save our lives.
I didn't rush to try to save my
marriage.
I took an edible that my friend had
made and sent with my wife's friend
who came to remove my wife from
my life and return her back to
Atlanta where the players play.
We stocked up on nonperishables.

I stocked up on no fucks to give.
If you're not careful, not giving a fuck
can actually still take up a lot of
space.
I went into a semiconscious, numb,
trancelike state.
My default operating mode kicked in.
I went to work.
While my fingers began flying across
the keyboard to hurry and secure
housing for myself for the next day,
my mind began managing what this
separation would look like . . .
Okay.
She would need approximately six
months to two years to sort herself
out.
We will need approximately three to
six months to sort ourselves.
Good thing every American has three
months' worth of emergency savings
stashed away.
We'll be fine.
Things will be back to normal by
Christmas, and as always, we'll have
ourselves a merry, white one.
The question we asked ourselves,
How would we occupy ourselves until
things returned to normal?
How would we survive?
Rapidly, we were fixated on our
screens, devices, and televisions.
Marathon-watching the news.
Around the globe,
Reports coming in about the numbers
of the dead,

The rise in the numbers of the infected,
    the hospitalized, and the dying,
Contact tracing and blame tracing,
Black folx exclaiming, "I think I already
    had the Rona last fall" . . . always
    followed by a story of when they got
    that really bad cold that they couldn't
    get rid of all the way for weeks.
Journalists and media outlets turned
    death tolls into visually appealing
    and digestible charts and graphs.
Numbers, there were so many numbers.
And then it started . . .
The people that we knew started to
    talk about someone they knew who
    had caught the virus,
And then COVID-19-related deaths
    began to touch the homes and
    families of people we knew.
Jobs vanished.
Unemployment skyrocketed.
Businesses closed.
So many businesses.
People were scared
And hurting
And desperate.
In a system designed for the white and
    affluent
We poor Blacks saw the same fatality
    rates with COVID-19
That we saw in every other sector of
    this Black American life

As the targeted, marginalized,
    vulnerable racial group.
When the whites suffered,
We suffered more.
The suffering came in waves,
Repetitive.
With windows of fear open
We were constantly being lulled by the
    sounds of the COVID-19 death
    waves.
We were rocked with disbelief
    seasoned with spicy despair.
It stung like salty tears in our eyes,
But after a while, it numbed,
Our rational brains taking on what
    our fragile hearts could no longer
    bear.
We would work our way through this,
And work would come in many forms.
We could plan and organize and
    manage it.
We were scrappy Americans.
We were Black, so our DNA was to
    survive this and come out on the
    other side even better than we
    went in.
But normalcy would not return
For me or for America.
For some, the American heartbreak
    was just beginning.
For others, we had seen America
    disappoint us before.

FOURTEEN

Reparations and Black Bereavement Time

In a capitalist society where every aspect of American life starts and stops by the almighty dollar, it is collectively understood and accepted that there are places where we must not speak too much about our Black grief, such as in the workplace. We save it for our homes and conversations with loved ones. Enslaved Africans were expected to work and to do so with little attitude, cheerfully even, to avoid the master's wrath. Production could not be interfered with no matter what slight the slaves perceived, even in the face of brutal violence and death. There was a place designated for us to express our grief: church. In the fields and in the big house on plantations, as a result of the grieving that we were denied, up from the voices buried in the ground rose old Negro spirituals, and we continue to sing songs of Black weariness, despair, and pain.

Black people have always made a way to express our grief. But even in modern times, we haven't fully examined collectively what we need to do in order to heal. America owes us reparations and Black bereavement time. With no place or time to care for our burdened Black hearts, we mentally and energetically count the dead Black bodies as they are piled on top of one another, repeatedly, for years. We are still waiting and hoping for relief as echoed in the words sung by our Black leaders during marches for equality during the civil rights movements of the fifties and sixties and today: "We shall overcome someday."

In consideration of what it would take to begin to facilitate the healing that needs to take place for us as descendants of enslaved Africans, please carefully read the words of the proposed act that would start a commission to study and develop reparations for Black Americans. This would be a tremendous step towards truth and reconciliation for this nation.

ARTIFACT

Commission to Study and Develop Reparation Proposals for African Americans Act

H.R. 40A BILL

To address the fundamental injustice, cruelty, brutality, and inhumanity of slavery in the United States and the 13 American colonies between 1619 and 1865 and to establish a commission to study and consider a national apology and proposal for reparations for the institution of slavery, its subsequent de jure and de facto racial and economic discrimination against African Americans, and the impact of these forces on living African Americans, to make recommendations to the Congress on appropriate remedies, and for other purposes.

Be it enacted by the Senate and House of Representatives of the United States of America in Congress assembled,

SECTION 1. SHORT TITLE.

This Act may be cited as the "Commission to Study and Develop Reparation Proposals for African Americans Act".

SEC. 2. FINDINGS AND PURPOSE.

(a) Findings.—The Congress finds that—

(1) approximately 4,000,000 Africans and their descendants were enslaved in the United States and colonies that became the United States from 1619 to 1865;

(2) the institution of slavery was constitutionally and statutorily sanctioned by the Government of the United States from 1789 through 1865;

(3) the slavery that flourished in the United States constituted an immoral and inhumane deprivation of Africans' life, liberty, African citizenship rights, and cultural heritage, and denied them the fruits of their own labor;

(4) a preponderance of scholarly, legal, community evidentiary documentation and popular culture markers constitute the basis for inquiry into the on-going effects of the institution of slavery and its legacy of persistent systemic structures of discrimination on living African Americans and society in the United States;

(5) following the abolition of slavery the United States Government, at the Federal, State, and local level, continued to perpetuate, condone and often profit from practices that continued to brutalize and disadvantage African Americans, including share cropping, convict leasing, Jim Crow, redlining, unequal education, and disproportionate treatment at the hands of the criminal justice system; and

(6) as a result of the historic and continued discrimination, African Americans continue to suffer debilitating economic, educational, and health hardships including but not limited to having nearly 1,000,000 Black people incarcerated; an unemployment rate more than twice the current White unemployment rate; and an average of less than 1/16 of the wealth of White families, a disparity which has worsened, not improved over time.

(b) PURPOSE.—The purpose of this Act is to establish a commission to study and develop Reparation proposals for African Americans as a result of—

(1) the institution of slavery, including both the Trans-Atlantic and the domestic "trade" which existed from 1565 in colonial Florida and from 1619 through 1865 within the other colonies that became the United States, and which included the Federal and State governments which constitutionally and statutorily supported the institution of slavery;

(2) the de jure and de facto discrimination against freed slaves and their descendants from the end of the Civil War to the present, including economic, political, educational, and social discrimination;

(3) the lingering negative effects of the institution of slavery and the discrimination described in paragraphs (1) and (2) on living African Americans and on society in the United States;

(4) the manner in which textual and digital instructional resources and technologies are being used to deny the inhumanity of slavery and the crime against humanity of people of African descent in the United States;

(5) the role of Northern complicity in the Southern based institution of slavery;

(6) the direct benefits to societal institutions, public and private, including higher education, corporations, religious and associational;

(7) and thus, recommend appropriate ways to educate the American public of the Commission's findings;

(8) and thus, recommend appropriate remedies in consideration of the Commission's findings on the matters described in paragraphs (1), (2), (3), (4), (5), and (6); and

(9) submit to the Congress the results of such examination, together with such recommendations.

SEC. 3. ESTABLISHMENT AND DUTIES.

(a) ESTABLISHMENT.—There is established the Commission to Study and Develop Reparation Proposals for African Americans (hereinafter in this Act referred to as the "Commission").

(b) DUTIES.—The Commission shall perform the following duties:

(1) Identify, compile and synthesize the relevant corpus of evidentiary documentation of the institution of slavery which existed within the United States and the colonies that became the United States from 1619 through 1865. The Commission's documentation and examination shall include but not be limited to the facts related to—

(A) the capture and procurement of Africans;

(B) the transport of Africans to the United States and the colonies that became the United States for the purpose of enslavement, including their treatment during transport;

(C) the sale and acquisition of Africans as chattel property in interstate and intrastate commerce;

(D) the treatment of African slaves in the colonies and the United States, including the deprivation of their freedom, exploitation of their labor, and destruction of their culture, language, religion, and families; and

(E) the extensive denial of humanity, sexual abuse and the chattelization of persons.

(2) The role which the Federal and State governments of the United States supported the institution of slavery in constitutional and statutory provisions, including the extent to which such governments prevented, opposed, or restricted

efforts of formerly enslaved Africans and their descendants to repatriate to their homeland.

(3) The Federal and State laws that discriminated against formerly enslaved Africans and their descendants who were deemed United States citizens from 1868 to the present.

(4) The other forms of discrimination in the public and private sectors against freed African slaves and their descendants who were deemed United States citizens from 1868 to the present, including redlining, educational funding discrepancies, and predatory financial practices.

(5) The lingering negative effects of the institution of slavery and the matters described in paragraphs (1), (2), (3), (4), (5), and (6) on living African Americans and on society in the United States.

(6) Recommend appropriate ways to educate the American public of the Commission's findings.

(7) Recommend appropriate remedies in consideration of the Commission's findings on the matters described in paragraphs (1), (2), (3), (4), (5), and (6). In making such recommendations, the Commission shall address among other issues, the following questions:

(A) How such recommendations comport with international standards of remedy for wrongs and injuries caused by the State, that include full reparations and special measures, as understood by various relevant international protocols, laws, and findings.

(B) How the Government of the United States will offer a formal apology on behalf of the people of the United States for the perpetration of gross human rights violations and crimes against humanity on African slaves and their descendants.

(C) How Federal laws and policies that continue to disproportionately and negatively affect African Americans as a group, and those that perpetuate the lingering effects, materially and psycho-social, can be eliminated.

(D) How the injuries resulting from matters described in paragraphs (1), (2), (3), (4), (5), and (6) can be reversed and provide appropriate policies, programs, projects and recommendations for the purpose of reversing the injuries.

(E) How, in consideration of the Commission's findings, any form of compensation to the descendants of enslaved African is calculated.

(F) What form of compensation should be awarded, through what instrumentalities and who should be eligible for such compensation.

(G) How, in consideration of the Commission's findings, any other forms of rehabilitation or restitution to African descendants is warranted and what the form and scope of those measures should take.

(c) REPORT TO CONGRESS.—The Commission shall submit a written report of its findings and recommendations to the Congress not later than the date which is one year after the date of the first meeting of the Commission held pursuant to section 4(c). . . .

SEC. 7. TERMINATION.

The Commission shall terminate 90 days after the date on which the Commission submits its report to the Congress under section 3(c).

SEC. 8. AUTHORIZATION OF APPROPRIATIONS.

To carry out the provisions of this Act, there are authorized to be appropriated $12,000,000.

FIFTEEN

Grief Is Intergenerational

About a week after my wife left, my oldest daughter, Chelsea, had a mental health crisis. She was at times incoherent and agitated; she wouldn't sleep, couldn't sleep. She was combative with her boyfriend and her roommates. She could talk, but she wasn't functioning in reality at all. It was clear she was suffering. She was no longer recognizable as our Chelsea. Naively, we thought that after a few days, she would be okay.

There I was in Gatlinburg, Tennessee, where I had rented a room after Dawn left, and Chelsea was in Waco, Texas. On the phone, I was trying to monitor the situation, reaching out to medical and mental health professional friends for advice and guidance, while her boyfriend and her roommates took turns watching over her because she couldn't be left alone. We were all scared, trying to take care of her as best we could.

After about four days, she was not getting better; she was getting worse. After an old family friend arrived to assist her, Chelsea was admitted to an in-patient program. I got a call from the hospital at around four one morning as they were trying to get some basic information about her, but they wouldn't allow me to speak with her. I bought a plane ticket and drove five hours from Gatlinburg to Nashville to get on a plane to fly to Texas so I could be near her and available for whatever was needed. I checked into a hotel near the hospital where she was being kept.

The next day, May 25, George Floyd was killed by Minnesota police.

Since she was an adult, no one was calling to update me on my daughter's status. It took a few days to get her to sign the papers necessary for anyone on the staff to even speak to me at all, so I was getting most of my information from my ill child. According to what I was hearing from her and her nurses, she would be kept anywhere from a few days to a few weeks and then released once she was better. Since she didn't have a cell phone at the time, all I could do was wait, which mostly involved pacing, worrying, and praying by the phone in my hotel room so I could be available whenever she called me since I couldn't go to the hospital to see her because of COVID-19 restrictions. I hoped that this whole ordeal would be over soon, trusting and believing that she was in the best place she could be, where professionals knew how best to care for her.

Chelsea's time in the hospital was a miserable experience for her, and the details of all that took place, I'll never know. They discharged her with a protocol of care: prescriptions for antidepressant medications and outpatient counseling. I picked Chelsea up from the hospital, and by this time my other two children, Alexis and Adam, had arrived from Atlanta so they could support their sister, and so all four of us could be together.

We took Chelsea to her home in Waco, and that first night was great. With the four of us reunited and all together and with Chelsea back in her own surroundings, Alexis, Adam, and I tried to create a family cocoon for her. We laughed a lot, told stories, and reminisced about what life was like when they were kids growing up in our homeschooling household. We ordered takeout, sang, and danced. We talked about their dad, my ex-husband whom I had been married to for eleven years, Chaz, who had died suddenly back in 2016. This was the first time it had been just the four of us in a long time, and I really got a chance to revel and marvel at just being in my children's presence.

When Chaz died, pieces of my children splintered in so many different ways and directions that for the first time, I realized that as their mother I could not, in fact, fix everything for them. I certainly couldn't fix this. I had known the death of a parent when my mom died of non-Hodgkin's lymphoma in 2005, so I knew to some extent that grief would have its way with them and do whatever it was going to do. But these kids that Chaz and I had brought into this world, these new grievers, were so young at the time, only sixteen, seventeen, and twenty, and their youth seemed to make them too fragile for this kind of loss.

When I gave birth to Chelsea in a hospital in Arlington, Texas, as an unwed nineteen-year-old, Chaz was a new soldier in the US Army, finishing up his basic training at Fort Lee, Virginia. He would arrive a few weeks later, before his deployment to South Korea, to hold our baby girl for the first time as a new and enthusiastic twenty-two-year-old father.

When I gave birth to Alexis, Chaz and I had just gotten married a few months earlier, and he held my hand as I pushed her flimsy six-pound, four-ounce body out of mine. He was the first one to hold her, and a picture that captured his moment of new dad joy, as he gingerly held Alexis in his hands and gazed adoringly at her, remains one of my favorite memories of him.

After I gave birth to Adam, at the same hospital where his sisters were born, Chaz would tell the story of my labor, which he found to be hilarious. The contractions hit me hard, and I was in so much pain that upon arriving at the hospital, as he helped me walk down the hall to my birthing room, though we were taking the tiniest of steps while I gripped his arm tightly, I yelled at him to *"SLOW DOWN!"* and this would forever be relayed by him in a very funny and dramatic manner. I found his retelling to be endearing even if it was exaggerated. It was the kind of story husbands tell of their birthing and delivery experience that gives them a fixed place in the event, a way of emphasizing that they had an important role in the birthing process, too, which was being yelled at by their laboring wife.

He was there. He was there for all three births of our children, whether in spirit with Chelsea (which I felt in every fiber of my being) or in the flesh as he was with Alexis and Adam.

But now he was dead. And I was alive and here with our three kids, our bunnies. And now instead of having both of us in moments of crisis like this, they only had me. And I didn't feel like I was enough.

They say kids don't come with an instruction manual, but ever since the three of them were born, I always felt an innate sense of knowing how to be their mom, as if I had been waiting my whole life for them to arrive. Life as Chelsea, Alexis, and Adam's mom just made sense to me. But when their father died, for the first time

I felt utterly helpless and useless as their parent. I felt inadequate. I felt almost ashamed, embarrassed even, to be alive, to be the parent who survived. Maternal instinct failed me for the first time. I felt that all I could do was observe them, watch in horror as they stood side by side, holding each other's hands in front of his coffin, while I sat in the pew behind them, masking my own strange and confused, ex-wife grief, as my wife held my hand and rubbed my arm.

When Chaz died of a heart attack at the young age of forty-two, so many unhealed things came up for all of us. Chelsea's mental anguish was partly a manifestation of those ancestral and familial wounds. This is why all of us coming together during Chelsea's time of mental health crisis was so important to us. The four of us hoped that in some way, we could just be present with each other, the way we were when Chaz died, and everything wouldn't necessarily be okay, but at least we had a starting point, a returning point.

We grounded ourselves in one another.

We didn't know what to expect with Chelsea's mental health, but the second night after being released from the hospital, she had another episode that was scary for all of us. That's when I realized this was bigger than something that could be fixed with hugs from mom and little brother and sister.

I found a private facility that would accept her and got her checked in. This time when I picked her up from that hospital, we never left the parking lot. We fought horribly and said ugly things to each other. I wondered what the remnants of the scars we produced that day would look like in our future.

Sadly, we fell into old patterns of her being on the offense and me being on the defense, with little sleep, no patience, and too much trauma that we had both been carrying for years. I felt incapable of being there for her, and now I was unwanted by her. After this colossal argument, I called an Uber to take her back to her home in Waco where her brother and sister were waiting for her. She and I couldn't be in the car together, couldn't share the same space, and couldn't share the same air with each other because we had contaminated it with our angry words.

My baby girl slipped through my hands.

SIXTEEN

Grieving Is the Starting Point to Getting Free

Grieving murdered Black people woke me up to the reality that in a nation where our lives were being taken so frequently and recklessly, we were not free. As I considered the loved ones who would grieve for those in the Black community that we had lost due to state violence, I realized that I could no longer embrace the lie of American freedom. That was a harsh truth that I needed to grieve, coming to terms with the fact that the country that I loved didn't, in fact, love me back.

So my starting point to healing, even before my decision to finally leave America, was when I understood that as Black people, we have so much to grieve in our past, but also in our present. Just like death, grieving is a part of living. If we seek to honor ourselves, honor our precious Black lives, we will find ways to gently hold ourselves and one another as we grieve. If we are getting free, then our grieving must be a significant part of that. Telling the truth about the loss we have experienced and acknowledging the pain and hurt we feel opens a path to our freedom journey . . . and tears are always a part of that trail that leads us from what was to what will be.

We must say goodbye in many different ways, over and over again. Our tears can offer us some of the release we need to make space for the new grief that will settle in our spirits. We must not be afraid to grieve what we lose, whether the loss is chosen or not. Our tears can serve as a reminder to us to be soft with ourselves and the things or loved ones that we used to hold. As we move through the sadness of loss, reclaiming our tears can be an act of radical self-love that will carry us through our grief to our pathways of healing.

Grieving is sitting with the raw and real emotions that arise in our bodies, in our hearts, and in our minds. There is no bypassing or sidestepping grief. We can try to fight it, deny it, try to control or manage it, but it will show up however and whenever it will, whether we are ready for it or not.

Grief will have its way, and it must. Our presence with our grief can be a gentle, even beautiful, opportunity to reclaim our sadness around what or who it is that we are grieving and allow it to lead us to healing waters. We must allow our grief to wash over us, again and again, as often as it needs to, in order to become a part of who we are.

We must learn to integrate grief into our lives as the loss becomes a brand-new part of us. We will never again be who we were before we experienced the loss. We must choose to care for the parts of us that mourn the loss in a patient, compassionate, nonjudgmental, and loving way.

If we allow it, grief can renew our will to live.

Grief is both an ending and a beginning. It uncovers the truth of who we are, beyond what we say about ourselves. We may try to hide from grief. We may pretend that grief is not present. But we are only putting off the realization that grief is what allows us to honor the thing or the being that we once held.

Grieving reminds us that this body and this life have both finite and infinite truths. A finite truth is that people die and things come to an end. An infinite truth is that nothing and no one can take away the memories and the moments and the magic of things and loved ones that impacted our lives.

Grief can transform us. The grieving version of ourselves is a reminder that there is something to heal from, and if we are mindful to respect all parts of what is true about us, we can find gentleness and grace to honor whatever it was that we lost, and choose to take it with us as we go . . . or leave it where it is.

SEVENTEEN

Find Movement Every Day

Move your body. Dance, swim, fuck, walk, hike, anything that will get your blood flowing, your heart pumping faster, your body FEELING things . . . sweating, heavy breathing, endorphins releasing, whatever will get you out of your head and into your body.

As a retired fitness professional, I'd like to present my "Second Impeachment Proceedings Workout." Complete as many reps of each step as you can, thirty seconds on, thirty seconds off. Here's the breakdown:

- "We told y'all" squat jumps.

- Single-leg "it's only four years, how much damage can he do?" walking deadlifts.

- Side-to-side "this was the most unshocking, unsurprising, and predictable conclusion to Grand Master MAGA's presidency" lunges.

- Alternating "fuck y'all's call for unity now" box jumps, which can be modified with "miss me with the blaming antifa bullshit" toe taps.

- Alternating straight-leg "this is EXACTLY who the fuck America is" hip raises.

- "Black Lives Still Fucking Matter" curtsy lunges.

Repeat this set at least twice—you know, like how some white people voted for that man twice. And whether or not you choose to use this particular workout, the important thing is to just move your body in some way today and every day to help release some of the trauma your body is carrying.

At some point along the way, I picked up walking. There were no directions, neither sensory nor digital, no maps, no Siri, no warnings, no "be careful when you're on that side of town." I let my grief feet carry my weary body because my heart could do no more carrying. My heart had broken under the weight of lifting heavy things, so I walked.

JOURNAL PROMPT

How are you going to commit to finding movement in every day?

EIGHTEEN

Sit with Your Anger

> To be a Negro in this country and to be relatively conscious is to be in a state of rage almost, almost all of the time.
>
> —JAMES BALDWIN

Anger has a place in the grieving and healing process. I reject the blanket statement that Black women are angry while also emphatically and simultaneously declaring that we are absofuckinglutely angry and we have a right to be angry. For too long, we have denied our anger to deflect the ways in which the idea of our anger has been used against us to disqualify and reduce us.

There was a moment during my grieving when my anger showed up in a fierce way to protect my inner child. Instead of judging my anger and shooing her away like I normally do, I saw what she was doing to try to protect me. I hadn't been protected in this way before, so I invited her to stay and sit with me awhile. We talked. I listened. I thanked her. I invited her to come back anytime she feels like she needs to handle shit that my softness and grace can't.

From our anger, beautiful things can arise. We are angry but we are also so much more. Our opportunity to get free lies in how we give our anger a space and a place and how we honor our anger as a valid and necessary part of our grieving and healing work. In order for me to move through my grief to a place of healing, I had to acknowledge and deal with my rage.

Sometimes it's okay to think that our anger is trying to protect us. However, it is more truthful to think that it's actually protecting something else that's a little deeper than that.

—LAMA ROD OWENS

I had so much to be angry about, having experienced the pain and devastation of being abandoned by my father at the age of forty for being queer, and then being abandoned by my wife after almost eight years together. I understood the sadness and endless tears, as those were emotions that made sense to me. It wasn't until anger showed up that I felt out of control and worried about not being able to manage my emotions. I was afraid of the fire that was burning in me.

When Breonna Taylor was murdered by the SWAT team, my first reaction was rage. Grief didn't follow any neat stages or structure; I went straight to feeling that my anger would consume me, fueled even more when no one was held responsible for her death. This was very much the same way I felt after the video of Ahmaud Arbery being gunned down by easily identifiable men went viral, and upon hearing that they had not been arrested but were still walking around living their free, racist lives for nearly three months after murdering him.

My anger was so visceral that the taste in my mouth changed to sour and my heart must have hardened. It is when the temperature of my tears is hot that I know there has been a shift in my body, warning that I need some intervention to settle my being.

They say that fear is excitement without the breath. But anger felt like fear without the breath.

A POEM ABOUT KINDNESS AND ANGER

Antiracism is not about kindness.
Antiracism is about Black lives.
I am not a kindness educator.
I am not a kindness facilitator.

I am not even a kindness advocate
    when it comes to antiracism.
I am an antiracism educator.
My work is about Black lives.

I am an educator, facilitator, and
    advocate for Black lives.
I am a Black life.
That is what qualifies me.
I am a Black life.
That's what my work is.
I am a Black life.
My life is my work.
My work is my life.
My life and my work are about
    liberating my Black life and
    liberating all Black lives.
My work is not about kindness.
My work is not about white people.
My work is not about white people
    being kind to Black people.
There are too many white people
    focused on kindness and not
    focused on Black lives.
There are too many white people
    focused on having "tough
    conversations" about being kinder
    to everyone instead of being
    focused on saving and securing
justice and liberation for Black
    lives.
Antiracism work is not about kindness.
The work I do is not about niceness.
The work I do is not about all races just
    being kind and nice to each other.
Fuck kind and nice.
My work is about saving, valuing,
    honoring, respecting, centering,
    healing, fighting for, demanding
    justice for, and liberating Black
    lives.
I do not host yoga trips to
    Montgomery about kindness.
I do not host antiracism trips to
    Montgomery about kindness.
I do not host trips to Montgomery
    about how all lives matter.
I host yoga trips to the lynching
    memorial in Montgomery.
I host antiracism trips to the fucking
    LYNCHING MEMORIAL.
There is no kindness in lynching.
Quit talking to me about nice.

NINETEEN

Run Away

I made an intentional decision to go on hiatus for a specified period of time where I could be in a place of solitude and create space for my grief, where I could face it and hold it and find ways to honor it. As a nomad who literally didn't have a home, I was able to run away to San Francisco so I could create a plan that would enable me to heal and focus on doing things that would restore my spirit and my sanity and renew my will and ability to live.

I ran away so I could get help. I ran away so I could get still and listen. My body, mind, and heart had been working on overdrive, trying to process trauma on top of trauma. I had reached a breaking point.

I was homeless and alone. I struggled to get out of bed while also struggling to sleep. I knew how fragile and terminal my mental state was, so I knew that I had to use drastic and dramatic measures to get back to a place where I could cope. It wasn't possible to hold space for my grief while simultaneously continuing to show up as an organizer, facilitator, and educator, which is why I went on hiatus.

Not everyone will have the desire or resources to go on a physical hiatus. For those with limited means or ability, other forms of hiatus can include sitting for fifteen minutes in your car in the parking lot or driveway before entering the job or the house. Maybe it's putting the phone on airplane mode for an hour that you dedicate to reading about and mentally visiting, exploring, and dreaming of new places.

If going on hiatus is resonating with you, I offer an affirmation of encouragement that if you feel compelled to make a way out of a "no way," please believe that you can make your hiatus happen. Get creative. Make a plan. Ask for help. You can absolutely figure it out.

TWENTY

Make Space to Grieve

Going on a physical hiatus isn't necessary, though, or the point. What is necessary is that you acknowledge that you must take radical measures with regard to creating space and time to grieve and heal.

One of the tools I received from therapy during my hiatus was this activity on how to turn various experiences with loss into gems: gifts received from those experiences, tokens of something precious that once existed. I learned that I could make a conscious choice to take the gifts, the sweetness of those moments, with me on my journey of grieving, healing, and liberation.

ACTIVITY: THE GEMS THAT GRIEF GIVES US

Give yourself closure by creating a grief ceremony. Select a location. Make a list of the people, relationship, circumstances, or events that you need to grieve. Name what gem (a gift or insight or lesson) you got from whatever or whomever you are grieving. Select something to represent the gem (like a stone, which you may even want to keep on an altar). Give gratitude for the gem. Take a full, deep cycle of breath: long, deep, full, slow inhale; long, deep, full, slow exhale (listen to your body and repeat these breath cycles as many times as you need to). Let the tears come, welcome them. Burn something to symbolize the loss (if you can do so safely). Offer prayers to the ancestors or to Spirit with whatever is on your heart. Let it go with a blessing. Repeat this ceremony as often as you need.

TWENTY-ONE

From Broken Hearts
to Divorces

After sending Chelsea back to Waco, I accepted an invitation to stay with a white ally friend who had attended my Legacy Trip earlier in the year. She had a large and beautiful home in the Cole Valley district of San Francisco, so she offered me full range of her home, which included having my own room, two bathrooms, the kitchen, and the dining and living rooms. When I arrived at her home, I turned the bedroom into an emotional art studio where I displayed my dirty laundry in the round linen hamper, my altar of precious mementos on the brick mantel of the fireplace, and my wet, tear-stained tissue on the nightstand next to the freshly cut flowers in a small crystal vase. This was my grief hiatus.

Some nights the moonlight filled the room along with smoke from the Marley strain joints I bought from the white boys at the dispensary legally selling weed while Black boys sat in jail for illegally selling weed. Because here in the USA, white means legal and Black means illegal.

June 21 is the anniversary of my mother's death. She closed her eyes on this side and summer came. This summer felt similar to that one fifteen years earlier . . . more death. Just in a few different forms.

My marriage to Dawn came to an unexpected end with a text message from her that I received in that very room, my grief chamber: "I want a divorce."

My oldest daughter and I reached an unfortunate point where we had triggered the shit out of each other so much that I was no longer able to offer her any support because my mere presence only served to escalate and exacerbate her delusion and aggravate her mania.

Was everyone's world falling apart, or was it just mine?

I love how I feel when I'm high, so San Francisco promised and delivered that for me. I had deleted my social media apps when I landed at the airport, so I didn't have any digital connection to what was going on around the country. I knew there were protests and marches and rallies and, in some cases, riots. The signs around me that gave me a sense of what the country was going through were actual signs on telephone poles, announcing the details for candlelight vigils in parks on manicured lawns with gourmet coffee stands and designer nature trails and a multitude of shades of skin, except for Black, picnicking and drum circling and where the hell were the Black people? I wasn't sure how I got there; I just knew that was where I was.

The question I was asking myself was how could all the bullets that entered Breonna's body find their way through the walls that I had so carefully constructed around my little family of my wife and kids?

My days looked the same for a time: sunlight waking me in the most luxurious bed of heavy white down comforter, stuffed just right, high-thread-count white sheets, white oversized pillows. Outside of my collapsing world, the days for Black folx also looked the same for a time: white people asking all dem questions . . . a seemingly unending and monotonous hum of what can we do, what can we do, what can we do. Tell us, oh Black ones.

Those days and weeks I floated on a cloud of purple, and sometimes lemon, haze through Golden Gate Park. I marveled at the feeling of seeing so much alleged white solidarity with the Black community while not actually seeing any Black people outside of the parking lots full of tents where they hid the unhoused population. Other than that, I encountered very few Black folx there, and judging by the overenthusiastic reaction of one Black lady, who smiled and waved excitedly upon seeing me (a gesture that I of course returned), I had to assume she hadn't seen many of us either. It seemed to be a melting pot of every race but Black, and everyone seemed as surprised to see me there as I felt being there. Was I just high or did all the cars coming from all the directions stop and bow in condolence as my Black life crossed White Ally Street?

A POEM ABOUT SERENITY

> God grant me the serenity to accept the things I cannot change, courage to change the things I can, and wisdom to know the difference.
>
> —THE SERENITY PRAYER

My courage has come in knowing that
     I can only change my location and
     my participation in this toxic
     relationship. I choose to leave.
Today, I accept that I cannot make
     America love Black people.
Today, I accept that I cannot make
     America stop killing Black people.
Today, I accept that I cannot make
     America pay Black people
     reparations.
Today, I accept that I cannot make
     America provide universal
healthcare or legalize weed
     nationwide or release anyone in
     prison for weed-related charges.
I can't make America care about gun
     control.
I can't make America give a shit about
     the climate and our planet that we
     are actively destroying with
     colonialism, capitalism, and
     corporate greed.
My serenity, my peace, is granted in
     my wisdom, my ability, and my
     faith to get myself fucking free.

TWENTY-TWO

Gather Your Spiritual Practices

When I started on my personal journey of unpacking my internalized racism, I relied heavily on things that brought me peace, comfort, and a sense of safety and security, such as my yoga practice. I used yoga asana, the physical poses and postures, to get out of my head and into my body. I used meditation as a way to feel deeper and connect to my breath. And I employed a variety of other spiritual practices that strengthened and uplifted me during my deep healing and growth work.

I am defining spiritual practices as any activity that you thoughtfully and intentionally engage in that connects you to who you really are on a spiritual, mental, and emotional level. We have bodies, but we are not our bodies. We have thoughts, but we are not even our thoughts. The best way to identify the part of yourself that spiritual practices serve is to consider what for you makes you feel most like yourself. Where is the part of you that holds the truth about who you are to yourself? Spiritual practices aim to nurture your truest being. What is it that makes you feel like you are at home with and inside of yourself?

Our spiritual practices help us celebrate and feel connected to who we are.

Think of the moments in your life when you have felt most true to yourself. Maybe it was when you were a child singing in the school choir, a memory that takes you, as an adult, to a sweet place in your mind. Perhaps it was the feeling after you created something with your hands, like art, or with your mind, like music, and you saw that it was good and pleasing to yourself. This is the pleasure of creation! Some people feel most alive being in nature, in the mountains or by the ocean, or observing a sunrise or a sunset. These are a few spiritual practices, but there are many.

Our ability to get free lies in gathering for ourselves and utilizing a collection of spiritual practices. I encourage you to take on one or all of these: breath (or meditation or prayer), stillness, and movement. Every day.

Spiritual practices are disciplines. As an activist, you need to take action. Intentional action doesn't often make space for itself. You must create it. You can be gentle and gracious with yourself about when you make the time and how much time you carve out of your days to spend with yourself, but it simply must be done.

There need not be a big fuss about it. Don't overthink this, just pick a span of time; start with ten minutes. It can be the same time every day or it can change depending on your schedule. But time must be created and time must be set just like you create and set any other appointment for anything else. This time is dedicated to your breath and stillness.

ARTIFACT
The Eight Limbs of Yoga

In their book *Meditations from the Mat: Daily Reflections on the Path of Yoga*, Rolf Gates and Katrina Kenison discuss the teachings of Patanjali, an ancient Indian Sage who was believed to author the Yoga Sutras and who some regard as the father of yoga. The Yoga Sutras are a collection of teachings on the theory and practice of yoga and are widely known for the yogic lifestyle framework, The Eight Limbs of Yoga. These teachings are the foundation for how to embody yoga in body, mind, and spirit.

Yamas: The Five Moral Restraints
Ahimsa: nonviolence
Satya: truthfulness
Asteya: nonstealing
Brahmacarya: moderation
Aparigraha: nonhoarding

Niyamas: The Five Observances

Sauca: purity
Santosa: contentment
Tapas: zeal, austerity
Svadhyaya: self-study
Isvara-pranidhana: devotion to a higher power

Asana: Postures

Pranayama: Mindful Breathing

Pratyahara: Turning Inward

Dharana: Concentration

Dhyana: Meditation

Samadhi: Union of the Self with Object of Meditation

TWENTY-THREE

Reclaim Your Time

We must replace the oppressive narrative about time being money with any number of liberating narratives, such as that time is precious, time is a gift. Even seeing time as a construct can be helpful when considering that we must make time for ourselves.

Living in a capitalist society, somewhere between being carefree elementary-age kids who think we have all the time in the world to play and that morning we start our first job, we are taught that time is money. The messages and narratives that we receive from media, from our families, from educational institutions, reinforce the concept that time costs money, and we internalize that. In traditional jobs where we work as employees for employers, whether hourly or salaried, we trade our time for dollars.

Today, Americans work multiple jobs, have side hustles, live with roommates, and/or have other nontraditional ways of living and earning money just to make ends meet. For many Americans, our access to rest and play time daily, weekly, monthly, and annually revolves solely around the jobs that we work and what our benefits packages look like.

According to data from the Bureau of Labor and Statistics, it can be inferred that for full-time, private industry workers in America:

- The average workload is more than forty hours per week.

- The average amount of sick or paid time off is seven days per year.

- The average amount of scheduled, approved, paid vacation is two weeks per year.

We literally don't have time. I don't even know how you've made the time to read this book (though I'm very glad you have). Most people will tell you that they don't have time. Don't have time for fun. Don't have time for hobbies. Don't have time to do the things they want to do with their lives.

And certainly no time to grieve or to go on hiatus or on a sabbatical.

If we are going to heal, and if we are going to get free, it is going to take time.

If we are going to get free, we must do as Auntie Maxine Waters said: we must "reclaim our time."

I cannot tell you where this time is going to come from. I cannot tell you how much time it will take. These are not questions anyone else can answer for you.

When we reach a place of desperation, when we find ourselves totally and completely helpless and lost, when we get to the point where we don't think we can go on, when we feel that we are at the edge of our lives and if we don't do something we may die, we perhaps can begin to look at time a bit differently.

Are you at your edge?

I was. And therefore, I had to reclaim my time.

JOURNAL PROMPT

Have you given yourself time to grieve when you've needed it? In what ways could you reclaim your grief time now (or within the next thirty days)?

* * *

ARTIFACT
Grieving and Healing Playlist

1. "Hymn of Healing" performed by Beautiful Chorus

2. "Ex-Factor" performed by Ms. Lauryn Hill

3. "Glory" performed by Common and John Legend

4. "A Change Is Gonna Come" performed by Sam Cooke

5. "Otherside" performed by Beyoncé

6. "River" performed by Leon Bridges

7. "Fool of Me" performed by Meshell Ndegeocello

8. "It's Okay" performed by Chandler Moore

9. "Strange Fruit" performed by Nina Simone

10. "Sunday Candy" performed by Donnie Trumpet and the Social Experiment

11. "Try Sleeping with a Broken Heart" performed by Alicia Keys

12. "Somebody Already Broke My Heart" performed by Sade

PART

II

Peace
and
Pleasure

TWENTY-FOUR

The Envelope in the Door

In November 2019, my wife and I were living in Little Elm, Texas. One morning, we were heading out for a walk by the lake nearby and upon opening the front door, Dawn found an envelope taped to the door, addressed to the homeowner of the house we had been renting for the past five months. It was one of those self-adhesive envelopes, so out of curiosity (and a little bit of suspicion), she opened it. Inside were papers with information about doing a short sale of the house we were living in. Over the past few months, we had been seeing things arrive in the mail from banks and people making offers to buy the house, which wasn't that unusual. But we still wondered if something was going on. The envelope in Dawn's hand was our confirmation. We were like, "Fuck, it looks like this house is about to go into foreclosure." It was at that moment that *Are We Free Yet?* was conceived.

We decided that instead of waiting until they informed us that the house was going into foreclosure and we had to move, we were going to be the ones to decide how this was going to go. We decided that we would move out, but only after we had stayed in the house a couple more months without paying rent, to take the time and save the money we would need to find somewhere else to live. With the house in some kind of foreclosure status, we felt that it was safe to assume that despite taking excellent care of the house, we wouldn't be getting back the double deposit that we had paid upon moving in.

When the country basically came to a halt in early March 2020, just a few months later, there was a prime opportunity for people to organize and address unfair housing practices on a large scale. Due to the global pandemic, a stalled economy, and millions of Americans losing their jobs, people faced evictions and foreclosures at all-time highs. Regardless of the number of Americans out of work and unable to pay their bills, banks still wanted their money, which meant that landlords still had their mortgages to pay, and as capitalism dictates, the people were discarded.

Receiving the envelope in the door was the moment when I decided I was done. I wanted a divorce from America. Losing our housing was only the latest hardship, but it clarified something for me about my life, which up until that moment had felt more or less "stable." I began to realize that the stability I had felt all my life was actually a mix of resignation and illusion. I had resigned myself to living a life of struggle, accepting the oppressive nature of capitalism, racism, and patriarchy as simply the way it was. I had grown not just accustomed to oppression but comfortable with it.

I had bought into the illusion of safety by participating in systems that were not providing safety (much in the same way that police officers do not make communities safe). At some point in my adult life, or maybe even earlier, I came to believe that knowing what to expect is the same as being safe. So that envelope in the door held more than just papers about a short sale. Those papers represented all the ways that capitalism and systems that support it were set up to keep me poor and in a constant state of anxiety about how I would pay bills and keep a roof over my head. Those papers illuminated how little value my queer Black life had due to the "bad credit score" that was plastered like a judgment of my character upon my chest. Those papers meant that though we were losing the thousands of dollars we had paid to the homeowners, we were discovering all the things we hadn't known about freedom, safety, and what it really meant to have a home. Turned out that home and safety were not where or what or who I thought they were.

JOURNAL PROMPT

Consider if you would participate in an organized national or local rent strike. Journal about why or why not.

TWENTY-FIVE

Unpack Your Relationship
with Anti-Blackness

When I say "unpack," I mean get to the bottom of what lies beneath the surface of your thought process and belief system, get to the root of what you internalize about the bullshit that keeps us enslaved such as, but not limited to, white supremacy, capitalism, and the patriarchy. A critical part of getting free and divorcing America is closely examining your relationship with the unjust systems that we have participated in, upheld, and perpetuated.

If we want to rid the world of anti-Black racism, we must begin by addressing and removing hatred toward Blackness within ourselves. Educating yourself about racism is a journey, and divesting from the effects of being socialized and normalized in white supremacy to prefer and trust whiteness is the road that will take you to addressing your own anti-Blackness. Once you see the ways that you have adopted harmful perceptions, stereotypes, ideas, and attitudes about and toward Black people, you will begin to see the oppressive systems that are in place, ones that serve racist functions and have racist impacts.

Our work to unpack our anti-Blackness lies in uncovering the racial bias that lives inside of us, unintentional as it may be, and replacing harmful anti-Black sentiments and narratives with truths about the inherent value, worth, and dignity in all of Black humanity. No less than anyone else. Then re-centering liberating truths such as Black joy, peace, and pleasure as tools of the revolution, understanding that our rest is resistance, that freedom must include everyone, and that the way to get there is by serving those most marginalized among us.

And while Black people can't be racist, we certainly can and do harbor and perpetuate other harmful and oppressive behaviors when we engage in colorism, homophobia, transphobia, ableism, and more. We all have deep work to do around unpacking the ways in which we uphold oppression.

JOURNAL PROMPT

Consider your relationship with oppressive systems.
What specifically do you need to unpack?

TWENTY-SIX

Unpack Your Relationship
with Capitalism

A contributing factor to what is making us sick (physically, mentally, and emotionally) is the heavy weight of capitalism. The stress that comes from worrying about how we will figure out a way to pay our bills is deadly. We always hear about the importance of being debt-free when we should also be talking about how living in a system designed to keep us in debt is literally killing us—and forcing poor and marginalized folx to go into and remain in debt just to survive.

The backs of Americans are breaking under the weight of the national and personal debt that keeps us physically sick, financially struggling, emotionally drained, and mentally defeated. The cycle is exhausting and dehumanizing. Capitalism is based on the lie that the harder we work, the more money we will make. Meanwhile, hard work has never equated to earning money (see slavery), and the cost of living in the Capitalist States of America is going up while wages are going down. In fact, as of 2022, the federal minimum wage is $7.25 per hour and hasn't changed since 2009. Still, inflation and corporate greed continue to rise. Essentially, we are still living in a sharecropping system where the American government allows us to live on their (stolen) land while keeping us dependent on their system to do so.

For generations we have been told that education is the way to freedom, but we need to look at what the pursuit of higher education actually provides us in a racially capitalistic society. For Black Americans there are racialized implications that make capitalism even heavier; the burden of student loans, for example, is borne unequally by Black college students. Student loan debt is one of the primary barriers keeping Black families from being able to create and maintain wealth.

My oldest daughter worked her way through college with multiple jobs and received grants, loans, and scholarships. After graduation she got a job making $54,000, at which point the IRS sent her a bill saying she owed $10,000 for taxes on the grants and loans she received to get her through college. So she wrote them a check for $10,000 and told me about it afterward. When I asked her why she had sent them all her savings, she said she had done it because she didn't want that bill hanging over her head.

When she suffered from her mental health crisis a few years later, she lost everything and could have used that $10,000 she had saved up. According to the Education Data Initiative:

- Black college graduates owe an average of $25,000 more in student loan debt than white college graduates.

- Four years after graduation, 48 percent of Black students owe an average of 12.5 percent more than they borrowed.

- Black student borrowers are the most likely to struggle financially due to student loan debt, with 29 percent making monthly payments of $350 or more.

- In 2007–2008, Black bachelor's degree holders were the most likely among their indebted peers to describe their educational debt-related stress as "very high."

This much we know: The Roosevelt Institute brief shows that canceling up to $50,000 of student loan debt per borrower would immediately increase the wealth of Black Americans by 40 percent. What power and incentive does the government have to increase Black wealth instantly by 40 percent? In the US, they have all the power and none of the incentive because capitalism doesn't want everyone free.

Capitalism wants only a small percentage of the population to appear to have financial freedom attained through good, old-fashioned "hard work" (more delusion). In capitalism, it is necessary only to show that there are a few cases where their system of exploitation "works," but this is as faulty as when it is implied that an innocent Black man who gets exonerated after serving decades on death row is an indication that the system works. As Anthony Ray Hinton, an innocent Black man who served thirty years on death row in Alabama, said in HBO's documentary, *True Justice: Bryan Stevenson's Fight for Equality*, if the system worked, he would have never been arrested and charged for a crime he did not commit in the first place.

The reality is that Americans, with and without degrees, are finding it harder and harder to land jobs that pay a living wage. Many Americans work two to three jobs plus a side hustle or two just to make ends meet, pay off or down debt, save money for retirement, and possibly take some time off for a vacation every year or two.

We must connect capitalism to our dying, to our preventable diseases, to our depression and loss of will to live, to our fighting for resources that are abundant and that should be available to all but that are strategically kept behind unreasonable financial and racialized barriers so that the uber-wealthy can hoard and the poor can just die off or starve. We must see that if we continue participating in capitalism without radical strategies for change, we will continue to be burdened by a profit-over-people model and continue to contribute to our poor quality of life and early deaths.

TWENTY-SEVEN

Unpack Your Relationship with Credit

True or false?

- Credit is king.

- Cash is king.

- People who have bad credit are bad with money.

- People who have bad credit are irresponsible.

- Credit scores are racist.

- Credit scores and credit ratings matter in countries other than the US.

For a lot of reasons, we had bad credit. When Dawn and I decided to move back to our home state of Texas, we started looking for housing but were constantly rejected. My wife spent all her free time looking at different apartment complexes and houses for us to move into, only for them to check our credit, see our low score, and tell us we didn't qualify to live there. And in capitalism that translates to we don't qualify to live.

Having bad credit makes it very hard to damn near impossible to rent a home and do many things to take care of and provide for ourselves in the traditional sense. Folx with bad credit have to create alternative strategies to survive, including searching for homeowners willing to rent to people with bad credit. For us, this meant paying double deposits and way more money in monthly rent than traditional renters (folx with good credit). This was a normal part of doing what we had to do to survive as people with bad credit scores.

After several failed attempts to get approved to move into apartment complexes and houses being leased by private owners, we found a beautiful rental house on Lake Lewisville. After they had rejected us once already, and we were out of options, Dawn wrote a heartfelt letter basically pleading with the owners to give us a chance, promising them that we would take impeccable care of their home. So with a double deposit they agreed, and we moved into a beautiful house and we absolutely did take impeccable care of it and enjoyed living there . . . until we got that letter in the door and everything turned upside down.

We had been struggling financially since we moved back to Texas that summer. Having just completed a coding boot camp, Dawn was now a software engineer making almost six figures. We should have been fine. But every time she got paid, we were paying bills and debt and then asking friends and relatives to loan us money for gas and food to get us to the next payday. It was ridiculous. I was teaching cycle classes at a local spin studio to make extra money. I even started driving for Favor (a local delivery service like Uber). We paused and looked at our situation and agreed that this *was not what life was supposed to be.*

We were thinking: This doesn't make sense. What's wrong with us that we can't make ends meet, making this kind of money? We started to open our eyes and our minds to see and understand things in a different way. On the basis of some of my experiences in social and racial justice work, it wasn't a stretch for me to begin to put all the pieces in place and come to the realization that all of this was a fucking charade. We weren't trying to be rich. We were just trying to live.

But we weren't alone. The envelope in the door was a real moment of clarity. We knew that other people, especially generations of Black Americans, felt trapped just as we did, stuck with their debt and their bad credit. We knew we weren't the only ones who were undone with all the extra hoops we had to jump through and the extra money we had to pay (but with no extra protections put in place) just to secure housing and survive day-to-day life in the USA.

Credit scores were made up in 1989, associating responsible people with having good credit and associating irresponsible people with having bad credit. It was of no concern that capitalistic and racist systems created hardships and difficulties in Americans' lives (particularly marginalized people) that forced us to sometimes make decisions that would put us in positions where our credit was negatively affected.

The impact of the credit system on marginalized communities—where people are already struggling to make ends meet, find affordable housing, have access to healthcare and childcare and jobs that pay a livable wage, etc.—has in many ways become another way systems work to keep poor people poor. Credit became just another form of oppression.

I no longer wanted to "buy into" (literally and figuratively) the system of racist credit scores. My credit was already shit, so this didn't feel like such a huge risk. I decided to go on a full-blown debt strike. And the first part of that debt strike was a rent strike.

TWENTY-EIGHT

Learn about Rent Strikes

rent strike (noun): a method of protest commonly employed against large landlords. In a rent strike, a group of tenants come together and agree to refuse to pay their rent en masse until a specific list of demands is met by the landlord.

I began the New Year of 2020 on a rent strike. Dawn and I had a great deal of anxiety about this decision. I went to bed each night the month we stopped paying rent wondering, What are they going to do, are they going to call the police, are they going to come and enter the home because it is their house? I was worried . . . who the fuck decides they're just going to live in a house and not pay rent? (Squatters. They are called squatters, and capitalism hates squatters.)

I remember thinking they could walk in the door at any time and throw our shit on the street. We definitely had moments during December where we were like, "What the fuck are we doing? Can we really do this?" But the situation we found ourselves in felt completely unfair and reinforced so many other systems that weren't fair either. I wanted us to stand up for ourselves in some way. I decided that if we were going to start living differently, this was a risk we would have to take. This was an exercise of moving past our anxiety, discomfort, and fear.

We took a great risk and decided not to pay any more rent and to move out of the house at the end of January. We didn't announce we were doing this. We just didn't pay rent on December 1. After that, we wrote them a letter saying that it had been brought to our attention that the mortgage was not being paid. Therefore, in lieu of paying rent, we would take the steps necessary to find other housing and in order for us to do that, we wanted them to use our deposit as rent for the next two months, December and January. And then we would leave, without our deposit.

The homeowners reluctantly agreed to our terms. We stayed in the house and began working on *Are We Free Yet?* We had always talked about traveling the world once the kids were grown and not dependent on us, so we decided it was time, as my adult kids were out on their own and living their lives. We began the process of getting rid of everything . . . selling and throwing out and giving away all of our belongings. All of December 2019 and January 2020 were spent selling everything we owned: Craigslist, Nextdoor, Facebook, neighbors, friends. We gave away everything except a few boxes of personal and family items that went into storage.

TWENTY-NINE

Create Radical Strategies for Your Own Personal Liberation

I propose that in order to get free we invent new strategies for personal and collective liberation. The movement and struggle for liberation for Black folx collectively will always continue, and we need energy, focus, and strategy to get there. But at the same time, we need to expand our ideas around personal liberation. We need to adopt the idea that in freeing ourselves individually, we help the collective get free. And we need to encourage and support radical attempts toward liberation, such as going on rent, debt, and credit strikes.

But each time we as Black folx create new strategies for liberation, the US creates new strategies for oppression. What options do we have other than to get more radical with our tactics? And where collective tactics to free ourselves have failed, whether due to lack of planning or organization or participation, we must attempt our own tactics to free ourselves . . . by any means necessary.

Three reasons why Black people should not pay taxes:

1. Because the US government owes us Black folx reparations.

2. Because Donald Trump, Jeff Bezos, and other billionaires don't pay taxes.

3. Because the US Treasury Department and government officials decide how to spend our money/taxes to fund domestic and global destruction, imperialism, colonialism, exploitation, terrorism, and genocide, here in our own country, and around the globe. The US financially supports (with tax dollars and federal funding from the US Treasury, where decisions are made by appointed and not elected people) the increase and expansion of militarized law enforcement across the country, allowing the death penalty in twenty-seven US states, the killing of Palestinians by Israel, the corruption of the Cuban government, and countless other mass antihuman efforts around the globe. I no longer wanted my money going toward crimes against humanity that the US was and has always been responsible for and complicit in.

JOURNAL PROMPTS

- What are your thoughts about rent and debt strikes, and do you see these as being options for you? Why or why not?

- If the Divided States of Amerikkka were given a credit rating/score, what would it be? Why is or isn't this important to consider?

THIRTY

Let Go: Aparigraha

"A parigraha" is a Sanskrit word meaning nonattachment or non-hoarding, and basically describes the concept of letting go. In yoga philosophy, it's one of the "yamas" or ethical guidelines for interacting with the world around us, as presented in "The Eight Limbs of Yoga" and I consider this to be a part of my spiritual practices.

As Dawn and I prepared for our liberation journey, we decided to get rid of 95 percent of all our belongings. This caused us to consider what 5 percent we wanted to keep. Ultimately, I would keep only the humans I loved, the ones whom I gave birth to, the ones who invited me into their lives and their hearts and their stories. And the one whose ring I wore, who told me and made me feel every day that I was someone worth being, and worth being with. If I could let go of the stuff but keep the people, then surely I had everything I needed.

Day one after moving out of our rental house, I felt so free.

That was the last "home" that Dawn and I would have together.

They say live like you are dying.

Did we live February 2020 like it was our last?

It was really the end of the world as we knew it.

And we thought we were fine.

Another sacrifice that I made to let go and become a nomad was to carry and consume less. To maintain that spirit of aparigraha, I became a minimalist and began traveling and moving around with only one suitcase or checked bag, one carry-on, and one backpack.

I keep my possessions to a very few, which frees up space for me to live bigger when it comes to my full-time traveling lifestyle because I am not held back or down by stuff. Energetically and spiritually, being a minimalist causes me to be very intentional with everything, physical and nonphysical, that I choose to hold on to, and let go of.

AWFY PRO TIP

When considering planning strategies for moving abroad, start by reducing your monthly expenses. Eliminate some of those streaming services you have. Stop drinking gourmet coffee everyday. Buy less shit.

THIRTY-ONE

Nomad AF

A nomad is someone who doesn't have a permanent home but travels and moves from place to place.

Becoming a nomad was not a lifestyle that I had previously wanted for myself. Sure, I loved to travel, even as a kid. Summer vacations included trips to Disneyland and to summer camp and to visit our family in New Orleans and Chicago. I remember getting on airplanes as a little girl, loving everything about airports and flying—the holding of coveted plane tickets that I would later save in my scrapbooks, the crowded departure and arrival monitors displaying the locations of gates, which determined the speed and frenzy with which we would walk or run through terminals, the snacks that were smartly tucked away in our carry-on bags and also waiting for us mid-flight, and the collection of items in the seat back in front of us: barf bag, magazine, emergency instructions for dramatic crash landings.

But always knowing that I wanted to travel was different from deciding to travel as a way of life—one that went beyond wanderlust, in which moving around was a way to respond to not being free. As I looked around my life as a queer Black American woman living in the South, I saw and felt the heavy weight of white supremacy and capitalism . . . all the bills and debt that I didn't see ever making enough money to pay. I saw the disregard for Black life at the federal and state levels, in the institutions and systems from which we were supposed to receive protections and provisions. The vacations and weekend getaways I took as a stressed-out forty-year-old with unpaid balances looming over my head became only brief escapes . . . escape not from my mundane life, because life was anything but mundane, but from the system that worked every day to oppress us.

Travel was a financial splurge, a little fuck you to the creditors and institutions that were relentlessly calling my phone, demanding payment plans and threatening dings on my credit. On those three-to-ten-day vacations during the decades I spent working in corporate America, I dreamed of living my life like I was on vacation. I dreamed of being free, though I didn't have the language, or the courage, for freedom yet.

THIRTY-TWO

Finding Peace in Pain

The ancient Masters were profound and subtle.
Their wisdom was unfathomable.
There is no way to describe it;
all we can describe is their appearance.

They were careful
as someone crossing an iced-over stream.
Alert as a warrior in enemy territory.
Courteous as a guest.
Fluid as melting ice.
Shapable as a block of wood.
Receptive as a valley.
Clear as a glass of water.

Do you have the patience to wait
till your mud settles and the water is clear?
Can you remain unmoving
Till the right action arises by itself?

The Master doesn't seek fulfillment.
Not seeking, not expecting,
she is present, and can welcome all things.

—LAO-TZU, TRANSLATED BY STEPHEN MITCHELL

* * *

These words by Lao-tzu were foundational for me many years ago when I first committed to my meditation practice, helping me create a definition of what peace looked like for me on my quest to get free. And it was these words that I returned to over and over again when my life was the most chaotic, which served as a map to guide me to peace.

Making peace with our past can be painful and difficult. This is a process that will require time, forgiveness, tenderness, and care of your own heart. This is an area where having the guidance of a professional can be helpful. I turned forty in 2017, and that was when my father told me he would no longer be able to have a relationship with me while I was living in homosexual sin (being married to a woman), until I repented. So, with his ultimatum, I said goodbye.

The day before his religiously violent abandonment, I shared with him some conversations that I had had with my mother many years earlier about choices I was making that she believed meant I was "living in sin," such as when I moved out of my parents' house for a few months at age seventeen, and when Chaz and I lived together for a few months before we got married. My father was unaware that my mom and I had had these conversations, so upon hearing this information for the first time, he said that he fell under a heavy conviction that my mother was speaking to him from her grave, having always been the "better Christian" than he was. And so he regretted to inform me that he had been wrong and disobedient to the word of God by embracing me and accepting me all these years despite my "sinful lifestyle."

I was a grown-ass woman when my father disowned me for being gay.

I realize that not all Christians feel this way. But, people, check your faith. Check your devotion to Jesus or God or whomever you serve. And most of all, check your heart.

Ask yourself, where is the love?

This type of rejection happens to kids in Christian homes all across this world every day, in the name of Jesus. This type of mentality and theology keeps kids fearful in their closets so they don't get kicked out of their homes, harassed, or worse.

Peace can exist in the painful process of letting go, and even in the midst of conflict.

Having been disowned by my father, I had to learn how to operate from a peaceful place that moved through the perpetual pain that I felt. Losing my father remains both a dull and sharp pain, changing according to the seasons and situations of my life as a daughter who no longer has a father who wants anything to do with her. This loss feels active, unresolved in ways beyond my control. But my holding on to and prioritizing my peace by any means necessary gives me the strength and the patience to wait until the mud settles again. My peace practices offer a place for me to land when I am patient with this particular dynamic and with myself.

Protect Your Peace
at All Costs

Refusing to allow your peace to be disturbed is a non-negotiable. You can no longer afford to stay in relationships (or in countries) where your peace is unstable. Your community and your life can reflect the presence of more than just passive peace; peace can be active and engaged. For those of us who have marginalized identities who are working through family and religious abuse as we seek to make peace with our painful past, we must no longer accept such attacks against our personhood, and we can no longer afford to give our energy to people who refuse to see our full dignity and inherent worth and value. Stop giving people who do not value your humanity access to you.

You don't have to engage with toxic people, not on the internet and not in real life. Not even your blood relatives. Not even your country. Protecting your peace means setting and enforcing boundaries. Here is an example of how I responded when my father made another attempt to harass me over my sexual identity:

Good morning Daddy, how heartbreaking it must be for you and your God, your universal governor, to be separated from your children like this. I'm proud to be gay all day, every day. I consider it a blessing. The way you experience the words in your religious texts sounds more like a curse to me, so don't send me anything like this ever again. It is my hope that someday this will be a world where no one, no parent, no child, ever has to experience the separation and the hate and violence the way that I and too many of my other gay siblings have experienced. I am an awesome human with an awesome life who is surrounded by love all day, every day. It's disgusting that you continue to cling to this toxic ideology and behavior and poor treatment of your own daughter. I don't wish hell or anything bad on you, Daddy. That's not how love operates in my life. But I won't be harassed by you or anyone. Stop contacting me if this is the perverted version of "love" you are offering. I still don't want it.

Center yourself when setting your boundaries with a toxic person. You are the one experiencing their hatred and violence toward you. Say what the fuck you want to say, and sometimes you need to cuss them people out. Convincing, persuading, or getting them to understand your point of view shouldn't be the point. The point is to set clear boundaries and expectations to protect yourself. This is not an invitation for them to have a debate with you. You owe it to yourself to protect your peace above all else, and to remove yourself from toxic people and their toxic beliefs. If you don't protect you, who will?

For those of us with broken relationships with our family members, we have many questions that will go unanswered. No matter. We can still claim and receive forgiveness, healing, and liberation for them and for ourselves.

THIRTY-FOUR

Unplug from the Virtual and Digital Chaos

One of the biggest disruptors to our peace is digital media, with its constant pings and notifications and alerts and alarms and new methods designed every day to keep us plugged in and consuming information whether we are in a place to control what information we take in and when, or not.

I know you've heard it before, but you're going to hear it again now: put your devices down. Unplug from all the screens and devices and electronics and anything that diverts your attention from your senses. Schedule these times to unplug, in your days and in your weeks.

When you watch the news, remember to do so with caution. Be attentive and mindful about the media content you consume, and be intentional about validating and verifying the sources of information you seek out. Additionally, unplug from and unfollow social media accounts and influencers that make you feel less than safe.

Unplugging from sources that benefit from our full distraction is critical to staying in our peace. Turn your focus inward and create reservoirs of peace inside yourself. Once we establish what peace looks and feels like for us, we must prioritize and protect it at all costs.

THIRTY-FIVE

Make Peace with Your Past

After my wife left me, I made my way to my friend's home in San Francisco. A few weeks later, my wife reached out to me. We had been separated for about six weeks and the week prior, she had sent me a text message telling me she wanted a divorce.

By engaging in intentional grieving of our marriage and working with my team of therapists, I had arrived at a place where I could accept, and even agree, that we didn't need to be married to each other anymore. I still very much wanted to have my very best friend, my partner, in my life in some capacity. The marriage wasn't as valuable to me as our deep friendship and love for each other.

So when Dawn called me, I answered. And we talked for a few hours. We talked about what had been going on in our lives in our six weeks of separation, including about the people we were seeing at the time. She had recently met an "experienced poly" woman on a dating site, and I told her about the guy I was sleeping with and what I hoped would turn into a few new adventures on a threesome app. It was an easy conversation, just like all the conversations we had been having for the almost eight years of our lives that we had just spent together. It was natural. It was us.

At the end of our call, she told me that she was going on a weekend trip to Washington State for a plant medicine ceremony and she invited me to join her. I immediately accepted her invitation. She was paying for everything, so I booked my flight and prepared to meet up with her in Seattle in just a few days. There was no hesitation, no resistance, no anxiety, in getting ready to see her. There was only excitement and joy. She had been my person for almost eight years and I missed her.

In many ways, the therapy I had with Dr. Candice and her team of Black women therapists helped me let go of the relationship we'd had, so more than anything, I was looking forward to reuniting with Dawn to create our new way of being. I was experiencing a newfound sense of peace and felt happy and hopeful that I didn't have to lose my best friend, even though we would no longer remain married. It was a change I was ready to embrace.

A few days later, with a small group of folx, we traveled to a cabin in the woods of Cle Elum. When it came time for her to take the medicine, she asked me to come onto the mat with her. At first I told her no, I didn't want to impose on her very spiritual experience. I didn't want it to be about me or about us; I wanted her to fully receive whatever Spirit wanted to give to her without my interference. But she insisted I join her for her journey with the medicine, so I reluctantly agreed.

And I am so glad that I did.

In those moments, we held each other's hands and we cried. We released one another. To me, it felt like we were the only two people on this planet. While I can't fully put into words what I felt, the overall sensation was pure love. Love for one another. Love for everyone. Love for and from the universe.

The next day after the ceremony, we had our original matching tattoos, which we had gotten seven years earlier on the Las Vegas strip, refreshed with color splashes. It was meant to signify a death of what was coming to an end between us, and the adding of colors was to represent whatever we would become. We had a beautiful four days together. In some ways, we felt like we always had. We easily melted back into each other in many ways, including sexually. But it was also very tender . . . there was a lot of apologizing and hand-holding and long conversations, which had always been one of the most beautiful parts of our relationship. There wasn't any expectation of anything going back to the way it was. There was only excitement about what the future held for us in this new place. At the end of the trip, we said our goodbyes to one another and boarded our planes with excitement and anticipation for where our journey would take us.

Neither of us anticipated what would happen next. Her new, experienced poly girlfriend was upset with her for having sex with me.

The next day, Dawn informed me that she was going on a road trip with her girlfriend and wouldn't be available to talk to me for several days. She was on a mission to win the girlfriend back and wanted to spend all her time and energy and focus on her. So despite the ceremony and the intimacy we had just experienced, she couldn't communicate with me for a while. And just like that, I was discarded and abandoned all over again.

Over the course of the next three weeks, I would send my wife a dozen emails. I was searching for answers that only she could give me. I was looking for reason and reassurance. I tried making sense out of this matter of the heart.

This is where peace stepped in. I began to understand that this was what it meant to be fluid, shapable, receptive, and clear. Being as careful as someone crossing an iced-over stream meant that I would have to graciously and compassionately accept that though this breakup was painful, peace was mine to choose. This was another lesson for me in letting go. It would require time, gentleness, and patience for me to accept and make peace with this part of my life that was becoming my past.

JOURNAL PROMPT

Define what being at peace means for you. How does peace look in your day-to-day life, or how would you like it to look? How does peace physically present in your body?

THIRTY-SIX

Get Outside

Get outside, get to the water or the beach if possible. Fresh air, sun on your skin. Find nature. Find trees. Hug them. Ground yourself . . . take off your shoes, bare skin and bare feet directly on the land. Sit or stand with nothing between you and the earth. In the dirt, grass, or sand. Touch the land. The longer, the better. Incorporate getting outside in nature, getting to the water (rivers, lakes, beaches, or even just taking a shower) as a part of your spiritual practice.

THIRTY-SEVEN

WPP
(White People's Problem)

White supremacy is a racist system that interrupts our ability to get free. It is a system designed to empower and maintain the institutional and social privilege of the dominant racial group in America: white people. Convincing white folx that my Black life matters is no longer a priority of mine. It is only important to me that we Black folx get free and live in a way that demonstrates that we fully know and believe that our Black Lives Matter. There came a moment when I realized that in my attempt to rid the world of racism by calling myself an antiracism educator and facilitator, I was centering white supremacy in my life. Yes, the work to dismantle racism is necessary. Yes, we need Black antiracism educators and leaders. But when I stepped back from my antiracism work, I realized that by focusing on racism all the time, I was stealing sweetness from myself. The effect and impact of always discussing and explaining racism and white supremacy, of always teaching about the dynamics of oppression, was that I was removed from an empowered place of liberation.

The ongoing discussions about dismantling white supremacy had taken a toll on me. The revisiting and researching, the remembering my own stories of complicity and searching my own heart to find the ways that living in a white supremacist society shaped me and contributed to the parts of me that I was trying to get free from, the perfectionism, the self-judgment, the mental chaos, the repeated racial inflictions of engaging with white folx who might or might not yet be ready to personally take their antiracism journey from an intellectual place to a heart place where transformation happens, all of this was re-traumatizing over and over again and began to suffocate me slowly.

I realized that in my fight to tear down white supremacy, I was actually allowing the fight to tear me down. In centering my work, my time, my thoughts, my energy, my conversation, my constant focus on the thing that I didn't want (to exist in racist systems and structures), I was less connected to the thing that I did want (joy and liberation). And I was creating and re-creating the stories and scenarios of the evils caused by white supremacy. I was endorsing it simply by acknowledging its power. I was standing on the very hill that I wanted to destroy. What would I have to stand on instead?

It had become apparent to me, especially during the uprisings of the summer following George Floyd's death, that white people needed to take on a more personal commitment to dismantling racism inside of themselves, just as I had to take personal responsibility to unpack and divest from my own internalized racism.

It occurred to me that my ancestors didn't get free from enslavement so I could kill myself fighting white supremacy. I decided to build a practice of peacemaking by first being peaceful. I decided to shift my focus from what I didn't want to what I did want. I decided that I no longer wanted to talk and teach about racism in the ways I had been.

I decided that instead I wanted to educate, facilitate, and inspire around grieving and healing, and centering tools for liberation for Black folx. I was done with centering my work on talking to white people about racism (and other systems of oppression).

THIRTY-EIGHT

Team Blaxit

Blaxit (noun): the modern-day resurgence of African Americans who choose to exit the United States either primarily or in part due to systemic, anti-Black racism.

The term "Blaxit" was coined by academic, journalist, and human rights consultant Dr. Ulysses Burley III, who combined the words "Black" and "exit," a reference to Britain's Brexit.

I decided to Blaxit because as a queer Black woman, I could no longer afford to live in the United States. I don't remember exactly where I first learned about Blaxit, but in 2018, I started joining online groups of Black folx who were planning to live or already living outside the US. It was there that I found encouragement, inspiration, advice, and thought-provoking questions and considerations as I began planning to leave the US to live abroad. And so, Dawn and I were formulating our own Blaxit plan to join this growing Black social movement.

One post in an online Blaxit group read:

I've been talking to a friend about reparations and he's telling me that all African Americans who have left the US to live abroad have forsaken the struggle. He's saying that those of us who have left the country have abandoned our duty to our brothers/sisters in America. What do you all think?

My response was this:

This mentality believes it is our duty to struggle. It is not. This line of think-ing suggests that we somehow deserve to be oppressed and remain in oppres-sion just because our ancestors were. They didn't deserve it then nor do we deserve it now. If they could have left this land, they would have. Our ances-tors fought for our freedom and for some of us that will mean staying while making the best of it (as is your friend's choice) and for others, we are choos-ing to leave the plantation. None of our choices are free. Whatever ways we choose to get free came at the cost of our ancestors' blood and very lives. Our freedom to choose to Blaxit has already been paid for and I'm not waiting on reparations. The words of Assata Shakur (the OG of Blaxit) come to my mind: "It is our duty to fight for our freedom. It is our duty to win. We must love each other and support each other. We have nothing to lose but our chains."

ACTIVITY

Check out and follow these Blaxit platforms and influencers (and do a Google and You-Tube search to find more): Blaxit Tribe, Blaxit Global, Blaxit Radio, Stephanie Perry and vaycarious.com, Shida's On The Loose, Black Expats Living Abroad, Black Expats and Repats in Jamaica.

THIRTY-NINE

Black Americans
Who Moved Abroad

I t's important to note that anti-Blackness is global. One should not expect that leaving the US and moving to another country means that one won't experience discrimination, because that isn't the case. But what we find as Black Americans is that while no country is perfect and every place has its own unique problems and challenges, there is no racism quite like the American brand of racism, the racism that we have been born into and live with every day in the US.

The concept of Black people moving abroad to find a better quality of life is not new. Black Americans have been fleeing our places of birth in search of freedom since the days of slavery. As white supremacist terrorism continued to be pervasive in the South during the Jim Crow years, millions of Black folx relocated to the North, Midwest, and West in a movement known as the Great Migration. And it is in that spirit that we have the modern-day movement of Blaxit.

As we consider reasons why we may feel compelled to leave for another land in hopes of a better quality of life, we can learn from the many examples of Black folx who explained their decision to leave.

Excerpts from a letter from Frederick Douglass, Victoria Hotel, Belfast, to the abolitionist, journalist, and social reformer William Lloyd Garrison, January 1, 1846:

My Dear Friend Garrison:

I am now about to take leave of the Emerald Isle, for Glasgow, Scotland. I have been here a little more than four months. . . .

I can truly say, I have spent some of the happiest moments of my life since landing in this country. I seem to have undergone a transformation. I live a new life. The warm and generous co-operation extended to me by the friends of my despised race—the prompt and liberal manner with which the press has rendered me its aid—the glorious enthusiasm with which thousands have flocked to hear the cruel wrongs of my down-trodden and long-enslaved fellow-countrymen portrayed—the deep sympathy for the slave, and the strong abhorrence of the slaveholder, everywhere evinced—the cordiality with which members and ministers of various religious bodies, and of various shades of religious opinion, have embraced me, and lent me their aid—the kind hospitality constantly proffered to me by persons of the highest rank in society—the spirit of freedom that seems to animate all with whom I come in contact—and the entire absence of everything that looked like prejudice against me, on account of the color of my skin—contrasted so strongly with my long and bitter experience in the United States, that I look with wonder and amazement on the transition. . . . Eleven days and a half gone, and I have crossed three thousand miles of the perilous deep. Instead of a democratic government, I am under a monarchical government. Instead of the bright blue sky of America, I am covered with the soft grey fog of the Emerald Isle. I breathe, and lo! the chattel becomes a man.

As Josephine Baker said of her time in France, in the speech she delivered in 1963 at the March on Washington:

I could go into any restaurant I wanted to, and I could drink water anyplace I wanted to, and I didn't have to go to a colored toilet either, and I have to tell you it was nice, and I got used to it, and I liked it, and I wasn't afraid anymore that someone would shout at me and say, "Nigger, go to the end of the line."

. . . So over there, far away, I was happy, and because I was happy I had some success.

And James Baldwin:

You look for a place to live. You look for a job. You start doubting everything. You become sloppy, that's when you start to slip. All of society has decided to transform you into nothing. I knew what was going to happen to me, I'd kill or be killed. . . . I left because I didn't think I could survive the race problems.

Other notable Blaxits were made by:

Audre Lorde to Mexico (1954) and Germany (1984–1992)
Maya Angelou to Ghana (late 1950s–1963)
Alice Walker to Kenya and Uganda (1964)
Henry Louis Gates Jr. to Tanzania (1970) and England (1973)
Tina Turner to England (1987), Germany (late 1980s), and
    Switzerland (2013–)

JOURNAL PROMPT

Which of the previous quotes resonate with you? Write them in your journal and learn more about these Black Americans and why they left the US.

FORTY

Welcome to Jamrock

I had been planning a move to Durban, South Africa, and had some work lined up there. Then COVID-19 hit and that got canceled. I then shifted my Blaxit plans to Da Nang, Vietnam, because I had been watching and following the growing Black expat community there. But while I waited on Vietnam's borders to open up, a friend told me that Jamaica's borders were open.

I bought a plane ticket that same hour. Two days later, on July 24, 2020, I was there.

I don't think we talk about the emotional part of the divorce process enough. Divorce fucking hurts.

I loved Texas at one time. I loved the United States at one time. Very much. What I loved most about those places were all the people I loved who were wrapped up in them. And this is how it is with failed marriages. There is a lot of love there, but there is also an internal negotiation, for everything that feels funny, off, or not right. There are things that we tell ourselves make up for the nagging question of whether this was the relationship we wanted. There is justification for careless words spoken in a hurry and for perceived slights.

In December 2021, Texas passed horrendous legislation on abortion. In March 2022, Texas governor Greg Abbott used his power to harass and threaten trans children and their families. I have never wanted my fucking tattoo of that fucking state off my body as much as I did then. Love is wild that way.

I remember the marital wisdom and advice my grandpa Perkins, my mother's father, gave me early in my marriage to my ex-husband: "Just as long as the good days outweigh the bad, you'll be fine." My grandparents had been married for over fifty years before being killed in 2012 when their car hit a tree in Haynesville, Louisiana, where they had fled after losing everything in Hurricane Katrina. My other grandparents had also been married for over fifty years when my grandmother died in 2014, turning my grandfather from a doting husband into a widower.

Staying married is just what I watched my family do. Till death do us part. Staying is ancestral. Staying is American. Staying maintained the family structure, which was valued above all else, no matter how torn and tattered. We were to keep raising that worn-out family flag through countless battles of verbal attacks and silent treatments. But all too often what staying also maintains is the status quo, the resignation, the walking on eggshells, the codependency. Staying maintains the oppressive structures that depend on our compliance and participation. When we get married, it is with the smug and well-intended disclaimer that "we don't believe in divorce."

So we try to make broke shit work.

I will never forget something I heard Dr. Phil say on *The Oprah Winfrey Show* back in the nineties, which stayed with me into my own marriage that I thought was divorce-proof. And it was a quote that I wished my mother had taken into consideration, as she chose to stay with my father despite his emotional and substance abuse. "It is better for kids to come from a broken home than to live in a broken home." This was the decision-making factor when I divorced my ex-husband, wanting our kids not to live in a broken home with two broken people who were hurting each other and didn't seem to know how to stop. The decision for me to leave America was the same.

Sometimes, we forget that we are not trees; we can move. We have the choice to leave. Breaking up meant having to somehow find space to respect the woman that I was when I loved America, just as I found space to respect the woman I was when I was married to my ex-husband. We had grown apart and with the distance, and with eyes that began to open, I realized that I was in a toxic and abusive relationship with America.

It was simply time to go.

I ran into the arms of Jamaica and indulged in any and every pleasure so I could feel something, anything. And after I left America, everything felt good, especially in those first few weeks and months.

Jamaica was ready and willing to receive me, for a variety of reasons—I was American, I was woman, I was beautiful, I was smart. What wasn't there about me for Jamaica to love?

At forty-three, with three grown kids and heading into my second divorce, I decided to start my life over from scratch, and I chose to leave the US to do so. In America, I was falling, but Jamaica was there to catch me. And so it was there that I went to grieve and heal, telling myself and the universe: We got this.

Within the first four weeks of leaving the States and moving to Jamaica, I had all but forgotten about my home country, vowing that America would never again have my heart.

JOURNAL PROMPT

What would it take for you to Blaxit? If you had the means, where would you go? What are "the means" for you?

A POEM ABOUT PRIVILEGE, PASSPORTS, AND WEDDING RINGS

Upon leaving the States and landing
  in touristy Montego Bay, I
  learned that two of my most
  valuable possessions were my
  American passport and my
  wedding ring.
My passport was evidence that I
  belong to the promised land of
opportunity, the land flowing with
  milk and honey.
My passport signaled I had a piece of
  the fictional American pie.
My passport suggested that I was a
  dreamer of the American dream.
My passport was coveted by many
  Jamaicans and was the prize at the

end of the classic story of the American woman who falls in love with a Jamaican man who now has access to a country that otherwise would not readily or happily receive him.

My passport held greater value to those who didn't have it.

I gripped my passport with contempt, but I wasn't willing to throw it away.

Perhaps my landing in Jamaica allowed me to discover just how far removed from my homeland I wanted to be and didn't want to be.

My passport allowed me the freedom to go out and window-shop other countries, poke my nose inside foreign corner markets, just to look and see, then politely retreat to the next international venue that caught my eye.

My passport, along with my thick American accent, drew shop owners and beggars and street vendors and scammers.

They saw my locs and I was an empress.

They heard my voice and I was an American.

They saw my body and I was a toy.

Walking down the Hip Strip was like walking through a maze of Jamaican men, and I tried to mix a little hint of Jamaican accent into my one-word indifferent greetings so as to give the illusion that I wasn't American (or Canadian or British, for that matter).

But with my accent, there was no way I could be invisible.

At the most, my wedding ring provided a thin buffer between me and the Jamaican men whose noses were trained to sniff out potential American woman sponsors.

There is a running joke among Black American women that as soon as you look a Jamaican man in his eyes (or fuck him), you are in a relationship with him whether you know it or not.

I have never met a Jamaican man who does not possess a charming mouth dripping with flattering words.

You feel the heat of Jamaican men wanting you before you are within earshot of their slick and alluring pickup lines.

You had to take a stance of almost rudeness to escape the attention if it was unwanted.

But at least it wasn't America.

AWFY PRO TIP

Get your passport.

FORTY-ONE

Unpack Your Relationship
with Patriarchy

If you aren't trying to dismantle the manifestations of patriarchy (misogyny, homophobia, transphobia, etc.) then you aren't truly trying to dismantle the manifestations of white supremacy. They are directly connected and sustain one another.

—FREDERICK JOSEPH

Moving to a Black country like Jamaica allowed me a measure of peace in that the people I saw and interacted with on a daily basis were Black. I hadn't fully understood how the sensory experience of being surrounded by mostly Black people would settle my nervous system. What I loved the most about Jamaica was its unapologetic Blackness. Jamaican Blackness feels very different from American Blackness. The deep sense of Jamaican pride is present in all Jamaicans. Everywhere I looked I saw Black skin in varying sun-touched, sometimes bleached shades and varying shapes of Black bodies. Blackness in Jamaica is an attitude of great self-confidence. All Jamaicans seemed to possess an innate knowledge of self-worth and inherent value due to their heritage of resistance, from the history of the Maroons to liberation from England in 1962. All the smiles were Black.

The patriarchy is a looming menace to society. Sadly, I discovered that Jamaica was just as patriarchal as my new ex-country, if not more. Growing up as young American girls, we are conditioned in a heavily Christian-influenced society, which is set up to accommodate all the men around us, based on their racial hierarchies and power dynamics: preference and deference to cis-het white men first, then Black men. Humans who identify as women are socialized and indoctrinated to defer to men and their wants and needs above all else. We are taught, and all too often violently forced, to observe, learn, and anticipate the moods of the men around us because the expectation is that they must always be in a good mood so they don't blow up the spot. We learn as girls and women to walk on eggshells around men, to think, move, act, breathe, and cater to men in ways that center and prioritize them, ensuring that they experience maximum comfort and satisfaction, sometimes in order to keep the peace. Sadly, our ability to anticipate the needs of men is sometimes a matter of survival for women.

The saying goes, happy wife, happy life. And to a degree this can be true and play out in households where women are expected to hold everything—the responsibility of making and keeping everyone in the household happy—on their shoulders, which I learned in Jamaica should be covered in order to be respectable. Women are the holders of the temperature for the inhabitants of the home. We gauge where the men are and how they feel. We determine where the children are and how they feel. Our feelings, needs, and wants go overlooked and unmet as a function of our socialized gender roles, which are reinforced in conservative and progressive spaces, from marriages to commerce, from workplaces to dating habits.

Patriarchy operates in the same way that racism does. Rape culture thrives because patriarchal society dictates that women are here to serve the wants and needs of men. Purity culture exists because of men's unchecked obsession with dominating women, their sense of entitlement to own and possess our bodies and our sexuality. And the church wraps up our bodies, our virginity, our sensuality in ways that serve and support men as the heads of households and kings of castles.

FORTY-TWO

Learn about Misogynoir
and Intersectionality

Nobody's free until everybody's free.
—FANNIE LOU HAMER

As a Black queer woman on a personal journey of liberation, I need to name that I am also a Black feminist. That means that I center Black women (including femmes and non-men) and our inherent value, worth, and experiences related to the equality of all people. Black women are not just affected by sexism but also by racism and class. The interconnected, overlapping, intersecting, and interdependent ways that we as Black women endure inequality, discrimination, and oppression based on our gender, race, and class is called intersectionality, a term coined by pioneering civil rights scholar and writer Kimberlie Crenshaw in 1989. Being a radical Black feminist dramatically influences how I seek to get free. And in the same way that anti-Blackness is global, arriving in Jamaica reminded me that misogynoir is global too.

Let us also go beyond sexism (that all women and non-men experience) to understand misogynoir, a term coined by a Black, queer, feminist scholar Dr. Moya Bailey in 2010. Misogynoir combines the words "misogyny" (hating women) with the French word for black.

FORTY-THREE

Build Your Community

One of the saving graces in my nomadic journey has been the discovery of a community of Black expats that I have found in both Jamaica and Costa Rica. The good news is that these communities of Black expats exist all over the world. And we are actively working to seek out other Black people who share the same desire to leave the US, providing a welcoming and supportive environment so that we aren't on this Blaxit journey alone.

For those considering leaving the US but worried that they will find themselves alone in a foreign land, I can tell you that is not necessarily the case. Black people are everywhere.

Online Blaxit groups were how I met my dear friend Erica Watson, who walked off Facebook Messenger, where we interacted for the first time, and into my villa in Ironshore, which Erica and I would later dub "Black Melrose Place," partially because of some of my solo polyamorous pansexual adventures, but also because of the steady flow of visitors/characters who joined us there on our long-term stay in Montego Bay.

In this critical time when I felt so brokenhearted and unlovable, it was the new friends that I made, particularly in the Black expat online community, who lifted and held me up when I was at my lowest. And though I had only planned on staying in Costa Rica for a short trip for the purpose of a scheduled private retreat with my sex doula, Amina from the Atlanta Institute of Tantra and Divine Sexuality, I decided to stay longer because of the Black women community that I found here (and also because I had fallen in love with the country of "pura vida"—the pure life).

Black women have always been here to receive me.

Y'all. When you get divorced, you will lose some of your friends and possibly even some family. Going through a divorce can be a very lonely and depressing experience. And when it comes to leaving America, not everyone will understand or support you in making radical changes to your lifestyle, even if that's what it takes for you to get free. There were many people in my life who didn't understand my need to leave the States and didn't get my sense of urgency to save my life. In deciding to divorce America, I have sacrificed a lot, including my social circles and some friends. But I have gained so much and have learned that my path is my own and not everyone is called to walk it. Additionally, not everyone will be there to celebrate the peace and freedom that you find abroad. That is a reality that all divorcées, and expats, must accept.

I prepared myself for the loneliness I assumed I would experience moving to a whole new country. But that was far from the case. The experience of making Black expat friends and becoming a part of the Blaxit community (which includes Black folx all around the world) remains one of the most enriching and beautiful parts of my AWFY journey.

And the same can be true for you.

AWFY PRO TIP

Join online Blaxit groups and consider hiring an expat relocation specialist or service.

FORTY-FOUR

Get Queer AF

Queer not as being about who you are having sex with, that can be a dimension of it, but queer as being about the self that is at odds with everything around it and has to invent and create and find a place to speak and to thrive and to live.

—BELL HOOKS

There came a point when I realized that I was unlike my grandma Olivia in that I wasn't "proper" like her, but that didn't mean I was broken. It wasn't until I was in my late thirties that I first heard and adopted a word that described how I felt: "queer." "Queer" is a multifaceted word that is used in different ways and means different things to different people. Here are some ways that "queer" is used today (from the Queer 101, Unitarian Universalist Association blog):

1. **Queer (adj.): attracted to people of many genders**

   Although dominant culture tends to dictate that there are only two genders, gender is actually far more complex. *Queer* can be a label claimed by a person who is attracted to men, women, genderqueer people, and/or other gender nonconforming people.

2. **Queer (adj.): not fitting cultural norms around sexuality and/or gender identity/expression**

Similarly to the first definition, *queer* can be a label claimed by a person who feels that they personally don't fit into dominant norms, due to their own gender identity/expression, their sexual practices, their relationship style, etc.

3. **Queer (adj.): non-heterosexual**

    Queer is sometimes used as an umbrella term to refer to all people with non-heterosexual sexual orientations or all people who are marginalized on the basis of sexual orientation.

4. **Queer (adj.): transgressive, revolutionary, anti-assimilation, challenging of the status quo**

    Many people claim the label *queer* as a badge of honor that has a radical, political edge. Unitarian Universalist seminarian Elizabeth Nguyen has preached: "Queer, for many folx, is about resistance— resisting dominant culture's ideas of 'normal,' rejoicing in transgression, celebrating the margins, reveling in difference, blessing ourselves."

5. **Queer (n.): an epithet or slur for someone perceived to be gay or lesbian**

    Queer is still sometimes used as a derogatory term. Many people who have had the word *queer* used against them are understandably very uncomfortable with the word.

The way I experience the term "queer," in the simplest sense, is as a synonym for "different"; a deviation from what is considered the norm by a racist and patriarchal society. That difference is most commonly associated with sexuality, but as our dear ancestor bell hooks says, queer goes beyond sex. What society deems "normal" and what has been held up as the ideal, the preferred, the desired, and the ultimate standard is what is called "cis-heteronormativity." The opposite of that, or any way of being in opposition to that, is queer.

After accepting that I didn't come to this planet, to this life, to be normal or proper but to be queer, I was able to embrace my identity. In many ways, queerness for me was a gateway identity; by exploring it, I was able to unlock my feminism, which I had never understood apart from the context of my roles as a mother and wife. And it also enabled me to more fully and unapologetically embrace my Blackness.

The way that I was raised, Blackness was synonymous with Christianity. Everything Black about me and my Black family was centered on Jesus and the Bible and an active church life. So when I walked slowly away from the church and moved toward assimilating into whiteness in the corporate environment where I worked in fitness, I felt less Black. And likewise, the more I became disconnected from what was for the majority of my life a very close relationship with both sides of my Black Christian family, the less Black I felt.

But stepping fully into my queerness changed all of that. The more I embraced being queer, the more I was able to embrace ALL of me, including my Blackness. Seeing the ways in which my queerness freed me from restraints and constraints, I had the courage to step into the feminism I had always felt deep in my soul, which gave me permission to step into my Blackness as well. Being queer has been one of the greatest and most liberating gifts of my life.

FORTY-FIVE

Breaking Out of Cis-heteronormativity

I am queer out of necessity because cis-heteronormativity wasn't true for me. Cis-heteronormativity didn't allow for my creativity or expansion in the ways I wanted and needed to express myself and all the parts of me, especially the ways I was growing and changing from the woman I was in my early years as a mother and wife. Cis-heteronormativity was the box I was always designed to think outside of and break out of.

Being queer has taught me compassion for myself that I didn't find in the church or among the family I was born into. Having a queer heart allows me to love more humans and in more ways than cis-heteronormativity allowed. Having a queer mind has released me from the tight grip of linear, binary, academic, religious, patriarchal expectations. Being queer means that I am at the intersection of the intersections, not just Black, not just woman, but also not heterosexual. Where relationships are concerned, cis-heteronormativity offered me a trajectory from dating to monogamy, then marriage and monogamy, and finally, in my case as in more than 50 percent of all marriages, straight to divorce.

Cis-heteronormativity gives us purity culture and shame around sexual expression. It demonizes sex work while queerness validates, defends, and protects it. Cis-heteronormativity teaches us that it is the man who does the choosing, the initiating, the asking, the proposing, the leading, the providing, the "safety and security," and says that I, as a woman, am incapable of providing for myself because that is how God designed it. The man is the alleged giver. I lived the majority of my life believing that a benevolent and all-knowing and all-powerful God created me, a woman, for the purpose of helping men.

Cis-heteronormativity (particularly from an evangelical Christian point of view) dictated that I, as the woman, did the accepting, the responding, the answering, the following, the nesting, the submitting, the child raising, and the homemaking. The woman is the alleged receiver.

Cis-heteronormativity inside the church establishes an unsafe and insecure world for unmarried women because safety and security are offered and guaranteed and reserved exclusively for those who have a husband.

Cis-heteronormativity gave me the responsibility of managing the emotions, wants, and needs of "my man," and held me in contempt for "causing" his straying, his wandering eye, his temptation, his libido, his infidelity. When he was fucking up, I was counseled to pray harder for both him and me.

Cis-heteronormativity offered me greater value only when I was partnered in an exclusive, cis-het, monogamous relationship on the fast track to marriage. And as if I were racking up video game points, the more babies I had, the more value was assigned to me . . . the more years of marriage passed on the clock, the greater my value as a woman.

Cis-heteronormativity establishes a relationship hierarchy where the ultimate goal for all people is marriage and one of the greatest failures for a woman is being unwed, unchosen by a man. It dictates the value of relationships and friendships of any kind based on the presence or absence of sex.

Cis-heteronormativity in a religious sense required me to designate the majority of my time, energy, effort, affection, and attention to God first, to my husband second, and then to my kids. Despite countless hours, days, and years of biblical study on how to be a godly wife, I never did understand where I as an individual person was supposed to fit into the priority chart.

I'm not queer because my husband or I, or my parents, failed in any way, shape, or form. I'm not queer because I have daddy issues or because I have had "bad experiences with men." I'm not queer for any external reasons. I am queer because the fullest expression of who I am is in direct conflict with cis-heteronormativity and patriarchal gender roles.

A POEM ABOUT SEXUAL (R)EVOLUTION

When is the sexual revolution in your
    life coming
When will you allow your sexual
    awakening to take up space in every
    corner of your life
Turning your daydreams into tantric
    festivals
Your quiet moments into theatrical
    fantasies
Thanks to the patriarchy and purity
    culture
We learn to suppress our erotic
    feelings, thoughts, and desires when
    they arrive
By the time I got married to my
    husband at age twenty-one
I was stripped of any sexual identity
    that was my own
And given the *Little House on the
    Prairie* frock in its place
To be a Proverbs 31 woman
A suitable helpmeet for my husband
    (Black folx say helpmeet, white folx
    say helpmate)
From whom all blessings and curses
    would flow (as the old hymnals say
    in both Black and white church
    pews)
I remember looking at "single ladies" in
    awe
Literal amazement, almost

Wide-eyed and curious
What was it like to so badly want what
    I had
This coveted husband
Having the ultimate biblical prize
Meant that I was the ultimate biblical
    winner
Being able to submit to someone
A blessing
I was the good thing the scripture said
    my husband had found
The privilege to have a head of my
    household
Because a household without a head is
    dead
Like faith without works
And a headless house was worthless
As is a husbandless woman
When my kids were little
I was in several stay-at-home mommy
    Bible study groups
We met and used workbooks about
    being godly wives and mothers
We were taught to physically beat our
    children unto the Lord
So as not to spare the rod and spoil the
    child
But to train them up in the way they
    should go
So that when they grew old they would
    not queer from it

To teach us so we wouldn't be wicked
in the Lord's sight
To teach us how to pro-verb 31 properly
I was hand-selected to be the editor for
an online, conservative, evangelical
Christian newsletter
And I was invited to be a guest at a
conference for stay-at-home
Christian moms that took place in
Atlanta
I stayed at a nice white lady's house
And she served me a plate with sliced
red tomatoes next to a hunky side of
cottage cheese
The first time I had seen such a sight
And upon tasting it I decided that I
would include cottage cheese, like
whiteness, in my life
Therefore the assimilation continued
Because why not?
Though no matter what I did or how
hard I tried
I was never quite able to duplicate the
taste and texture of that moment
with my own tomatoes and cottage
cheese
I actually hated cottage cheese,
actually hated whiteness

But still, I looked for it in the grocery
store
But as a Black wife and mom of three
small children, I couldn't afford the
cheese of whiteness
We could only afford the cheese of
being Black and poor (which was
WIC cheese)
As the poor Blacks that we were,
the US government issued us
vouchers that designated which
cheese, which humanity, was
suitable for us
I never liked cottage cheese
Slimy and sticky
It comes with its own disgusting liquid
that it sits in
With chunks of not-quite-chewy,
not-quite-crunchy nonsense
That tastes like it's trying too hard to
have flavor that never quite
develops
Just like whiteness
Cottage cheese doesn't even get served
in respectable places
Because no one respects cottage cheese
Turns out I'm lactose and white
evangelical intolerant now anyways

FORTY-SIX

Unpack Your Relationship with Sexual Pleasure

For the last few years of our marriage, Dawn and I hadn't been having regular sex. Due to her own sexual trauma, we arrived at a place several years into our relationship where she didn't really want to have sex anymore. Though she swore and explained that it wasn't because of me, I internalized this. She insisted that she just didn't have any sexual desire whatsoever, didn't want sex with me or anyone else. It was just a place she found herself in as a result of her unresolved past.

In order to manage us properly, I valiantly agreed to a sexless marriage, reasoning with myself that our relationship was strong and was more than sex. I mean, as far as I was concerned, when we did have sex it was great, for the most part. But understanding what my wife had been through, I wanted to respect her needs and her feelings, and so I gave her space and assured myself that sex wasn't that important.

But after a few years, nothing had changed except the fact that I decided that I no longer wanted to sacrifice my sexuality and sex life. I felt young, just arriving at forty, and I still had a lot of sexual attraction toward my wife. I hadn't taken stock of what being married to someone who didn't want to have sex (with me) would do to my heart and my self-esteem and my overall sense of value and worth. I tried not to, but I took it personally, though I wouldn't understand that until after she had left me and we both began having sex with other people.

FORTY-SEVEN

Have Interstellar Sex

> Blessed are those who have been sent to be in the service of my healing.
> —TINA STRAWN

I wanted incredible sex for my forty-third birthday. So the gift I gave myself was joining a threesome app. After setting up a profile with six very hot pictures of myself, I immediately began getting responses and corresponding with couples and single men. Within two weeks, I had met up with six people and fucked three of them.

There was nothing ceremonious about meeting up. We already understood the assignment: interstellar sex. Our appetite for sexual pleasure with strangers was an important aspect to note because we knew and accepted what we were risking as far as our health was concerned in meeting up with and being sexual with random strangers during a global pandemic (this was July 2020, when I was still in California).

We were tapping into something beyond the real and present danger of COVID-19, plugging into the deeper, innate calling to touch and be touched and the need to prove that touch could feel like freedom. Could it also actually be freedom? I was committed to finding out. We shared the same craving for sexual exploration and the experience of new bodies to inhale and new skin to consume. We were drunk on love and sex. And nothing else mattered.

First, there was Ray. He was young, barely thirty. He met me at a park about a mile from the Airbnb where I was staying in Pacifica, an apartment attached to a house where the homeowner lived. We walked a bit, talked, sat down on a bench, and smoked some weed. I looked at his beautiful face, watched his perfect mouth, listened to his young-Black-man-raised-in-California voice, knew that once I kissed him I would know if in fact I wanted to fuck him or not. I basically said as much to him. He kissed me like he was deserving. And he was. So we did.

As a woman who had been separated, unwillingly, from her wife for only about six weeks, I was looking for new arms and I found them, easily and quickly. First with Ray, whose youthful enthusiasm pleased me greatly, whose eager touch excited me. He felt pure somehow, like the gift that he was, sent to me at such a time as this.

We were aggressive lovers and soft. His strokes often made me feel like I had to go to the bathroom, and I concentrated on the pleasure that it was, ignoring the body sign normal and natural in a human who previously had three babies sitting on her bladder. Back at that Airbnb apartment in Pacifica, I was sure the owner living next door heard us. We were so loud, and I kept telling myself to stop being so fucking loud but was not able to be quiet. It was his strokes of power that shook the entire apartment, headboard against wall, floor vibrating and all.

The owner's review of me after I left included a comment specifically about how quiet a guest I was, so that he barely even knew I was there. And I immediately wondered if that was his secret way of letting me know that he absolutely heard me.

A few days after returning from Washington, while Dawn was road-tripping and making amends with her girlfriend, devastated by the way she had casually discarded me, I fed myself with sex.

In addition to Ray, I met a young Colombian couple who were beyond proper lovers. We met up for the first time and sat on a picnic blanket sharing snacks and spliffs and small talk as the temperature began to drop and an invitation was extended for me to come back to their apartment. I accepted and for the next several hours, I belonged to them and they belonged to me, and our bodies danced freely and beautifully between one another.

FORTY-EIGHT

Increase Your Pleasure Capacity: Have More Orgasms

I acknowledge here that due to a variety of factors—including but not limited to physical disability, sexual trauma and abuse, and mental illness—self-stimulation, masturbation, and other forms of sexual self-care are not necessarily safe journeys for everyone. Carefully consider ways you can prioritize honoring yourself and the reality of where you are on your own path in exploring your sexuality. Having orgasms may not feel like a safe place for you. Please do whatever you need to do to get help specifically in this area. Be patient and gentle with yourself and give yourself permission to address whatever your discomfort or hesitation or resistance is around sexual pleasure and sexual self-play.

But what I discovered is that one of the most powerful ways to connect your liberation to your pleasure is through orgasms. If you feel stuck and unfree, perhaps you have a deficit of pleasure and orgasms.

Pro tip: orgasms are healing.

Spend time with yourself to examine and explore your orgasm, and if you pay very close attention to the sensations in your body during the process of attaining a heightened state of sexual climax, if you can zone in with laser focus on the pattern of your breathing and your own body's rhythm of increased arousal, if this feeling brings you to a state of bliss and ecstasy, then this is your sign to go further and deeper. If you can watch how your body feels, reacts, and responds leading up to, during, and immediately after having an orgasm, then you can map more ways to receive pleasure in your life, even beyond the sexual.

I am serious as fuck about my sex life and my orgasms. As I accepted the connection between spirituality and sexuality, I sought out and began working with my sex doula for the purpose of understanding my Ori, the inherent spiritual and sexual identity given to all humans at birth, on a deeper level. By honoring my Ori, I could unlock pleasure in all areas of my life. I know what unlocking my sexual expression did for me. When I understood and embraced myself as a worthy sexual being, who has a sexual personality at all times, when I acknowledged that there is no separation between my spiritual self and my sexual self, when I realized that being spiritually free had everything to do with getting sexually free, I understood how my liberation was tied to my sexual truths.

A common reason why we don't employ a pleasure practice is that we do not see ourselves as worthy. Another reason we don't prioritize our pleasure is that in a society that requires capitalistic participation, pleasure is disregarded and disrespected. Pleasure is a liability to oppression. Pleasure has no function in labor output. In fact, in order to maintain production, society needs to ensure desensitization. In order to push people past their need for pleasure and play, it needs to keep people exhausted.

When we remain busy, we remain unattached to our feelings. For example, play for the sake of playing isn't encouraged, but rather we are conditioned to use play and joy as rewards for hard work. When we reserve joy only for when we feel we deserve it, then we also justify the lack of joy in our lives as punishment for not working hard enough. By nature, many creatures work and play in some way to sustain their lives. And if we are lucky, we can "work" in such a way that it doesn't feel like work. Sometimes we tell ourselves that we love our work so much that it doesn't feel like work. This is a beautiful place to be in and we also must continually interrogate if that message serves us and our pleasure, or if that message has been co-opted by capitalism to indoctrinate us to work as a form or false sense of pleasure to replace actual forms of pleasure.

ACTIVITY

Listen to or read "Uses of the Erotic: The Erotic as Power," an essay by Audre Lorde, and journal what comes up for you. Afterward, use your fingers or your vibrator or grab your lover and explore and experience your orgasm. Repeat this escapade with your orgasm every day for seven days. Journal about it afterward. How do you think you might experience pleasure in your life if you prioritized your sexual self-play or orgasms?

A POEM ABOUT COCONUTS AND BEACHES

It is no small thing to find yourself
   walking alone on a secluded beach
   in Jamaica.
Alone Yet Brave was the new badge I
   was practicing wearing, as a single
   woman.
Knowing that I wanted more time at
   the edge of the sea, listening to and
   being in the water, I took a trip to
   spend eight days in Portland,
   Jamaica.
Each morning, after watching the sun
   rise over the watercolors from my
   mosquito-netted bed,
I would leave my bungalow and walk
   to where I would follow the wild
   cow trails down the dirt path,
   through neighbors' yards, gingerly
   stepping so as to miss the various
   piles of animal shit as the animals
   watched me suspiciously. Across a
   never-busy street that was
   frequented more by goats and
   people than by cars. Through the

yard of the large bar and grill, the
   open-air dining area, to the steps
   that led down to the sand. A few
   more paces and my toes touched
   rowdy Portland water that was
   better for looking at than for
   playing in.
The people of the town were early
   risers. Before the roosters, birds,
   and worms. So eyes watched me
   along my carefree and careless path.
   I walked the shore. The sea a lovely
   force to behold only. She would not
   welcome me into her waters. She
   was rough that way. Wade in up to
   your knees, maybe, because by the
   time you got out to your waist, she
   could overtake you like Jamaican
   drivers on two-lane roads. So my
   American feet were happy to stay
   close to the shore.
This particular morning, I found
   myself walking the water with my
   khaki pants rolled up to my knees,

my white tank top just an
unnecessary extra layer. So off it
came, tossed somewhere near the
restaurant. The flip-flops also were
weighing me down. So I left them
up against a crusty, worn-out
retaining wall.
Though I knew there were eyes
around me, I saw no other soul.
Long Bay Beach in Long Bay,
Portland, or Porti, as we locals
call it.
I set out to walk and pray and sing a
mile with the morning clouds,
Sun and water to my right,
Yards I walked through and ackee trees
on my left.
There is something sacred about going
to the water.
The spiritual parts of me have
known and felt this since I was a
little girl.
Since young, singing, "Take me to the
water to be baptized," as I followed
along with the choir,
Gathered among the members of the
church my dad pastored,
The oldest Black church in Palo Alto,
California,
These beings who seemed to make a
human circle of protection around
me.
I knew there was power here.
And so as I walked, I prayed,
And as I prayed, I walked.
I faced the sun and the ocean,

Tears streaming down as my eyes
prayed,
Words coming out of my mother
mouth,
Pleading for my child,
Begging for Chelsea.
I was standing on holy ground
And I was never as close to God
As in that moment where I spoke
deliverance over my child,
Spoke healing into her life,
Affirmed who she was when she was a
guest inside my body
Before I gave her a name,
Before she opened up her eyes and took
breaths outside of my womb,
Purposed in love,
Purposed by design,
Purposed to be here,
To stay with me a bit longer,
To journey on together.
May she be well.
May she be happy.
May she be free.
Before I knew it, I had come upon
some guys chopping down coconuts
from a tree nearby. I was a woman
walking the beach alone, wearing
only a sports bra and wet pants. I
did not blend in.
They noticed me and waved. Then one
of the guys began to approach me.
In his hand he held a machete.
I willed myself to breathe.
Relax.
You are not in danger.

He came up to me, machete in one
  hand, coconut in the other.
Gave me the biggest smile.
And asked me if I would like some
  coconut water.
His eyes signaled the kindness of all of
  Jamaica.
I returned his warm smile with Yes,
  thank you.
He told me he had a restaurant up the
  beach a bit more and invited me to
  have breakfast.
I asked him what he was cooking.
Ackee, cabbage, breadfruit, dumplin'.
I told him I'd love some breakfast.
He asked me to give him about an
  hour and then he'd have a feast
  ready for me.
I told him to take his time, I had no
  plans other than to walk my beach
  laps.
So he took off to gather the ingredients
  he needed to cook.
And I resumed my gratitude prayers
  and water walking.
When it was time, I made my way to
  his restaurant.
Which I can best describe as the most
  charming shack restaurant I have
  ever been to.
Probably the best in the world.
Mac, the restaurant owner and chef who
  had approached me on the beach,
  had a group of friends with him.
Sturdy and slim, stocky yet rugged
  Jamaican men of varying ages that

you could never guess just by
  looking at them.
A school of mix-matched tropical fish.
About five of them hung around the
  small three-room shack.
And they adopted me into what I
  gathered to be their typical beach
  day. I was one of them now. And so
  was Daniel.
Does there need to be consideration
  taken when you have sex with
  someone of a different
  socioeconomic status than you?
When I fucked Daniel, I was not
  thinking about how much money he
  made or what he did to provide for
  himself.
Not. At. All.
I was thinking about the classic,
  signature Jamaican confidence that
  lured me into letting him kiss me
  passionately within hours of
  meeting him,
Feeling him press his body into mine
  impolitely and purposefully,
Feeling his pressure against my back
  just like I was feeling his hot breath
  in my ear, whispering, asking,
  confirming:
I know you feel the energy between us.
Fuck yeah I felt it.
It felt like the wet pants I was wearing
  that had dried while I sat with
  Daniel and his friends in the
  restaurant shack on the beach,
  singing American pop songs like

"Lose You to Love Me" by Selena
    Gomez, while smoking spliffs as a
    tropical rainstorm passed over us
As though the barometric pressure
    from the clouds had dissipated over
    us and gathered between my legs.
So he followed me outside the hut
Where I leaned playfully up against
    the walls of the flimsy structure
And fully took him in with my
    senses,
Received his mango-sweet Jamaican
    lips and tongue
That tasted as inviting as they looked,
And that was all that mattered to me
    in those seconds of decision
When in my head I traveled from
    restaurant shack to my
    mosquito-netted bed,
Willing my neural pathways to draw
    the lines to get us there,
So excited that we quickly left my
    flip-flops and our Jamaican gaggle
    of friends.
Down the beach,
Past the waters where I had prayed,
Up the dirt path made by wild cows
    and their chains,
Up to my premium bungalow
In the middle of the afternoon
Where I let Daniel take me
And he was masterful
Moments after we had removed one
    another's clothes,
Almost as soon as I had felt his
    grabba-stained lips

On my tart, sandy skin
My first thought of ecstasy was
    HOW???
How could he feel, and be, this damn
    good?
How did his hands know where to find
    the exact location on my hips to
    hold and guide me to willing
    submission (so THIS was what the
    elder mothers meant when they said
    when we found the right man, we
    would WANT to submit to him)?
How could he know how to roll his
    tongue down across my torso like
    that?
How did his warm Porti mouth go
    straight to my pulsing, throbbing
    clit so gracefully?
Like the grace I prayed back at
    Grandma Olivia's kitchen table in
    Chicago,
Like amazing grace how fucking sweet
    the sound
That saved a fucking wretch like me.
I had asked him back at the shack how
    old he was.
He proudly declared twenty-five,
But I was already drunk in
    lovemaking, so it mattered little.
We rocked the boat for a few hours,
Took a break at some point to relieve
    ourselves and get some water and
    smoke
Only to resume with me sitting on the
    edge of the bed
With the perfect view of the water

As I watched the sun go down while
    smoking a spliff that he had rolled
    for me
While he was thoroughly and orally,
    almost dutifully, occupied down
    between my legs
And I imprinted these images into my
    mind where they will be
    immortalized
As also now in this book
Because that's just the kind of fucking
    recognition sex with Daniel
    deserves.
So you see
I wasn't thinking about our
    socioeconomic status.
What is money even?
Well this is where capitalism meets
    the happy and oblivious couple
    in bed
Because fucking him for hours one
    afternoon in Portland was one thing
But wondering if I would like to have
    him in my space in MoBay to
    continue to enjoy having sex with

him and to see if there was anything
    more there
Was another thing entirely.
I had to look to my finances.
Could I include in my budget
A trip for Daniel to come and be with
    me?
He did not have the funds to sponsor
    himself on such a trip.
He had no money for the bus ticket
Or the food
Or any of the expense that would be
    required to support a
    five-day-and-night escapade with
    me back at Black Melrose Place.
So I calculated
And realized that this would be great
    fun for both of us
And I wanted us to have that,
I wanted to give that to us,
I wanted to give us a chance
And didn't want money to be the thing
    that kept us from literally fucking
    around and finding out
So I sent for him.

FORTY-NINE

Pleasure Power Principles

It is a radical thing to suggest that our work should feel like an orgasm. However, we must confront why we have placed restrictions on how much pleasure we can feel. Whom does it serve for us to not think of work in terms of pleasure?

If you woke up every morning with the purpose of maximizing your pleasure, your entire way of living would have to change. How much of what you are currently doing in your life would be eliminated if you led from a position of pleasure?

The secret is that our power lies in our pleasure. When we can feel and own our pleasure on multiple levels, we are able to step fully into our power. That is our radical act.

Your orgasm can tell you what pleasure feels like. Your sexual arousal, stimulation, and climax where all of your senses explode in an ecstatic rush of good sensations that consume every part of you is the X on the treasure map.

Does your work feel that good?

If not, why not?

Does the concept of your work feeling like an orgasm bring up resistance in you?

Why do you think your work shouldn't feel that good?

Who would benefit if your work felt orgasmic?

Who stands to lose if you begin to demand that your work must feel like you're about to cum? What if you delighted in your work, what if you sought out work that excited and stimulated you? What if you did not restrict your arousal, your best feelings of being alive, to specific moments that take place for short spurts of time during masturbation or lovemaking?

For us as humans, experiencing pleasure is more than an ability we possess. Experiencing pleasure is our birthright.

The problem isn't that your work doesn't bring you orgasmic pleasure.

The problem is that you don't *expect* your work to bring you orgasmic pleasure.

FIFTY

Take a Nap

Take a nap now. Put down this book. Go and lie in bed or on your couch or on the floor. If you have someone you want to make love to, make love. Or touch yourself. Or fall asleep. Take this moment to rest, beloved. Rest in all the pleasure you deserve.

ARTIFACT
Peace and Pleasure Playlist

1. "Holy" performed by Jamila Woods

2. "God Morning" performed by Natalie Lauren

3. "Affirmation: I Am Enough" performed by Coax Marie

4. "Faith" performed by Skip Marley

5. "Go Bravely" performed by Londrelle, Shelly-Ann Gajadhar

6. "When I'm in Your Arms" performed by Cleo Sol

7. "Stand Still" performed by Sabrina Claudio

8. "Into Orbit" performed by Alex Isley

9. "Summer 2020" performed by Jhené Aiko

10. "Lockdown" performed by Koffee

11. "Bloody Samaritan" performed by Ayra Starr

12. "Blessed" performed by Juls, Miraa May, Donae'o

PART

III

Celebration
and
Joy

FIFTY-ONE

A Brief History
of Black Celebration

Allow me to take you on a brief journey through Black American celebration. From Mardi Gras to the homecoming battles at historically Black colleges and universities (HBCUs); from Negro spirituals to hymns; from R&B to hip-hop; from weddings and receptions where aunties and uncles gather on dance floors to do the electric slide, to cookouts and family reunions where picnic tables are filled with elders schooling the young'uns on how to properly and respectably play spades and dominoes; from funerals to the second line to the Southern tradition of the repast, when we, as individuals and as a collective, find our songs and our dances, and when we feed ourselves with the food of hope, history, determination, and victory, we find our liberation.

As a descendant of enslaved Africans, what I learned from my lineage and my people is that in a world that won't celebrate us, we must celebrate ourselves.

JOURNAL PROMPT

Name one or more cultural or community celebrations that are meaningful to you.

FIFTY-TWO

Find Your Voice

I believe that birds sing because they are free, and I believe the same is true for humans. That's why there are freedom songs everywhere. Our ancestors left us bread crumb melodies in musical stories to help us find our way home to ourselves. In examining the ways in which we feel or don't feel free, let us start by acknowledging that it is our own truth that we must follow. Whether we write or sing, or both, we must find our voice.

Truth seeking and truth telling are ultimately acts of courage and faith. The more we listen to ourselves, the more we will recognize and trust our voice, which is imperative for both our liberation strategy and our liberation celebration. But following the beat of our own drum requires bravery in that we must be willing to sing for ourselves. Not speaking about our pain and our struggles prevents the healing that needs to take place. Not speaking about our triumphs and our celebration prevents us from leaving some notes behind for those who will be looking to follow in our freedom steps. We must find and use our voices to speak boldly and unapologetically, first to ourselves and then to those being drawn to our liberation tunes. Our silence is where our unfreed selves hide and remain hidden. Our silence serves oppression.

But where there is music, the captives are set free. When we use our voices and bring forth songs, we will find the power to break free. Let this be our affirmation to sing new songs of freedom.

ARTIFACT
"Lift Every Voice and Sing"

by J. Rosamond Johnson and James Weldon Johnson
(also known as The Negro National Anthem)

Lift every voice and sing
Till earth and heaven ring,
Ring with the harmonies of Liberty;
Let our rejoicing rise
High as the listening skies,
Let it resound loud as the rolling sea.
Sing a song full of the faith that the
    dark past has taught us,
Sing a song full of the hope that the
    present has brought us.
Facing the rising sun of our new day
    begun,
Let us march on till victory is won.

Stony the road we trod,
Bitter the chastening rod,
Felt in the days when hope unborn
    had died;
Yet with a steady beat,
Have not our weary feet
Come to the place for which our
    fathers sighed?
We have come over a way that with
    tears has been watered,

We have come, treading our path
    through the blood of the
    slaughtered,
Out from the gloomy past,
Till now we stand at last
Where the white gleam of our bright
    star is cast.

God of our weary years,
God of our silent tears,
Thou who has brought us thus far on
    the way;
Thou who has by Thy might
Led us into the light,
Keep us forever in the path, we pray.
Lest our feet stray from the places, our
    God, where we met Thee,
Lest, our hearts drunk with the
    wine of the world, we forget Thee;
Shadowed beneath Thy hand,
May we forever stand.
True to our God,
True to our native land.

FIFTY-THREE

Eat

It's critical that I give some of the credit and honor for my healing to the food that I ate from the blessed island of Jamaica.

The way I ate changed as I moved through different phases of my grief. Some days I received nourishment exclusively from a single protein shake. Other days I consumed only weed and water, the diet of brokenhearted queer Black girls who run away to Montego Bay. But there were days I allowed the joy from the mangoes and the avocados (which are called pears in Jamaica) to substitute for the void of heartbreak.

Sometimes when I missed Dawn a lot, I would sit in the kitchen at Black Melrose Place while Michele, the Jamaican woman who cooked for the guests at the property and who had become a dear friend, prepared her Jamaican meals, made for me with love from her own blessed hands, and I would close my eyes and remember my wife in the kitchen preparing food for me, with a love that I hadn't known had an expiration date.

I went from cooking for a husband and three kids, every day, for years and years, to eating the food she cooked for me, for years and years. She loved to cook, and I thought she loved to cook for me. Perhaps she did. The food she prepared for me tasted like she loved me. Every single time. And now, a new pair of hands prepared meals for me made with love, next to the Caribbean Sea. Michele spoke to me not in patois because I didn't understand it all the time yet, but I understood the plates of fruit she set in front of me: Soursop. Pineapple. Papaya.

I understood her love because it came in the form of my favorite meal of gungo soup, a rich soup made of peas, which became my new comfort food. Her hands made me food that would bring me back to life, getting something into my mouth and into my grieving body.

I took a picture of that first plate that Michele prepared for me, though I don't remember what food was on it other than rice and peas. I instinctively knew that at some point, I would want to remember what food sustained me.

ARTIFACT
Ingredients from a Jamaican Menu

"We no hav dat."

Bammy.

Breadfruit.

Callaloo

Festival (which I used to accidentally call "carnival" on occasion).

Plantain.

Jamaican patties.

Run down.

Sugarcane.

Grapes, which I used to get delivered weekly.

Ackee and saltfish.

The thing about ackee is that it's Jamaica's national fruit. It grows all over the island, reddish. It is poisonous while it is still attached to Jamaican trees. Only once it falls from the trees and breaks open does the toxicity leave and the fruit becomes safe for human consumption.

Of course I came to an island that grows poisonous fruit.

She was my poisonous fruit.

Fritters.

Escovitch fish.

Ground provisions, which are a starchy goodness staple traditionally served for breakfast in Jamaica, typically consisting of some combination of the following: boiled banana, yam, Irish potato, coco, dasheen, breadfruit, cassava, and dumpling pronounced without the hard g at the end. Also known as "hard food," it is the food of the slave trade legacy, brought to the island to feed the enslaved and too often starving African ancestors. Grounding, earth energy food . . . highly vibrational . . . comforting . . .

nurturing . . . dense . . . weighty . . .
big ooman ting!
Coconut.
Jerk everything.

Abba's Cuisine. Pier 1. Tracks and
Records. Margaritaville. Pizza Hut
MoBay. Devon House. Island Juices.
Jamaican KFC.

ACTIVITY

Take pictures of the food and meals you eat for a week. Then, in your journal, consider the following: What story does your food tell about your healing journey? About your joy and celebration? What are you serving on your liberation menu?

FIFTY-FOUR

Yoga Meals

Here is a practice that changed eating for me:

When I went through my two-hundred-hour yoga teacher-training program, back in 2012 during my fitness career, I learned about yoga meals. Eating a yoga meal means eating by yourself in a very slow and thoughtful way. We were encouraged to take small bites, only one at a time, to chew slowly and intentionally before swallowing, and to finish each bite completely before putting more food into our mouths. We were not to have any distractions while we were eating, not reading a book or being on the phone or talking to anyone. We were supposed to be thinking about the food we were eating, paying attention to the way it felt in our mouths, noticing all the flavors and the texture. We were to move the food around in our mouths to experience as much of each bite as we could. We were to think about our choice in food, where it came from, who prepared it and how, where it was sourced. We were encouraged to select natural foods, with as few added ingredients and preservatives as possible. We were encouraged to think about how eating the food made us feel. We were to engage mindfully and thoughtfully in the action of eating. We were to take our time and not rush to the next bite or rush through eating for the purpose of moving on to the next activity. We were to give thanks for the food and for the hands that prepared our meal, even and especially if they were our own. As much as possible, we were to be present with ourselves and with the process of eating this meal.

This way of mindful eating was like making grace last throughout the meal; more than just words spoken to bless the food, this was a way of blessing the eating itself. Being thankful for the food. Praying over the way that the food was providing not just what our bodies needed but also what our hearts and minds needed. As we grieve and heal, we must learn how to eat for our hearts.

ACTIVITY

Schedule a yoga meal over the next week and journal about your experience.

FIFTY-FIVE

Comments Overheard While Eating in Costa Rica

T here is so much happening in my mouth and in my heart right now."

"This soup tastes like a cuddle."

"This is unforgettable, like I'm never gonna forget how this feels in my mouth right now."

"This is a meal you travel the world for."

"I would like to thank myself for ordering this."

"When the food is so good that you nod as you chew."

"This is the food you save humanity for."

"What do I want my last taste to be?"

"I feel like they shouldn't even give people a choice about which dessert. They should just announce we're serving dessert, you're welcome, and bring this out."

"I want to take a picture with whoever made this so I never forget."

"Excuse me, can you tell me who is responsible for this?"

"The chef could get it."

FIFTY-SIX

Soul Food Stories

Every aspect of the making, serving, and eating of food is part history lesson and part love language for liberation activists. Soul food has been healing and nourishing our Black families and communities for generations. Poverty and religion, sorrow and celebration are ingredients that are baked into our food heritage stories, and as liberation activists, we can follow our inherited recipes, along with our memories, to create new meals, and joy practices, served at our tables of liberation.

Early in my first marriage, my father-in-law came to our home for dinner. I baked tilapia with a can of cream of mushroom soup on top of it, along with spaghetti with just sauce, no meatballs or ground beef or anything. I also made a salad consisting of just tomatoes, cucumbers, and pickles, mixed with Italian dressing, something I had seen my aunt in New Orleans make. I will never forget him taking a bite and commenting that it tasted "interesting." My husband roared with laughter. I was humiliated even though neither of them meant to hurt my feelings.

My husband explained to me that as far as he was concerned, spaghetti without meat wasn't actually spaghetti, it was just noodles with sauce, which was not a meal and certainly not fit to be a main course. I began thinking back to my mother cooking this meal of noodles and red sauce, canned green beans, and Jiffy cornbread. I didn't remember my father ever complaining or commenting on the meal, so my husband's announcement was new information to me.

It took me some time to realize that my cooking habits, which mostly came from my mother, sometimes demonstrated how poor my mom's family had been at times. And then I remembered some of the stories my grandparents had told me about when their seven kids were young and they were just trying to survive as a large family in that shotgun house near the Ninth Ward of New Orleans.

Grandma and Grandpa Perkins once told me about a time when they didn't have enough money to pay the electricity bill on time so their lights were cut off. But they didn't want their kids to know this. So, when the kids all came home from school that day, they were told that they would be having a very special dinner and would be eating by candlelight. They were instructed not to turn any lights on but instead to go and gather all the candles and bring them into the living room. My grandparents served the excited children dinner by candlelight as though they were in a fancy restaurant. The kids—my mom and my aunts and uncles—had the best time and never knew the electricity was turned off.

Let this serve as a reminder and encouragement to us to be creative and fun as we are designing our liberated lives.

When I became a wife, I asked both sets of grandparents to send me recipes that meant something to them.

Grandma Olivia sent me handwritten recipes in her lovely and proper cursive penmanship for candied yams and macaroni and cheese, things she traditionally baked and served to dozens for her famous Thanksgiving feasts. Grandpa Perkins typed out, double-spaced, his very detailed description of how to make gumbo. I treasured my mother's first Betty Crocker cookbook, which I had kept and saved through the years.

We must gather our familial stories in order to examine the ways that Black celebration has always been wrapped up in and around what we eat. Getting free involves reviewing all our ancestral recipes and gathering and eating rituals and making new ones to go along with our constitutions of joy and our declarations of liberation.

JOURNAL PROMPT

Write about one of your favorite family stories on the theme of food.

ARTIFACT
Variations on Beans and Rice

- America: red beans and rice. When I was growing up, red beans and rice was a meal that was commonly served in my family households in both Chicago and NOLA. Common ingredients are red kidney beans, white rice, spices and seasoning, and often some kind of meat like andouille sausage, typically left over from Sunday dinners.

- Jamaica: rice and peas. During my time living on the island, a staple food that was served everywhere was rice and peas, which is exactly like the beans and rice from my childhood (the "peas" are actually red kidney beans), but cooked with coconut milk.

- Costa Rica: gallo pinto. While I was finishing up this book, when I went to the local restaurants and ordered a traditional Tico breakfast (native Costa Ricans proudly refer to themselves as "Ticos"), it was always served with their version of beans and rice, made with other ingredients such as bell peppers, onion, and spices.

AWFY PRO TIP

If you choose to Blaxit or become an expat, commit to learning the language of the country in where you choose to live.

FIFTY-SEVEN

The War on Drugs

One of my favorite spiritual practices and ways of getting high is smoking weed. Known by many names including "pot," "marijuana," and "ganja," weed is a positive source of healing, peace, pleasure, and joy for people all over the world. As an effective and therapeutic plant medicine, it is used recreationally and for spiritual purposes and ceremonies, and it is widely prescribed to bring relief to those who suffer from various ailments. Weed is also a source of income for many.

For socially conscious people who smoke weed, getting high is an act of resistance because weed has been racialized and weaponized against Black people in the US.

The war on drugs, which is actually the war on Black people, was introduced during the Nixon administration and has not ended. And until every person currently sitting in jail or prison across the nation on marijuana charges is set free (as well as having their records expunged), the war against us won't be over and we won't be free. White folx sitting at the top of the multibillion-dollar cannabis industry while Black folx who have been arrested on marijuana charges fill the prisons is raging violent white supremacy in action.

Here are some of the factors to take into consideration when smoking weed, or advocating for weed legalization, in the US:

- Physical location: Am I in a state where it is legal to smoke or to be in possession of weed? Or am I risking a large fine, arrest, imprisonment, etc., if I get caught?

- Job risks: What are my employment implications and risks associated with drug tests? What would happen to my job if I tested positive for marijuana on a random drug test?

- Supplier: Where do I get my weed from? A street plug? Or a dispensary? Where does the money go? Who am I supporting?

- History and the law: What is the historical and current legislation on weed? Nationally as well as locally?

- Racial justice: What are the conditions for Black folx who are experiencing or facing incarceration for weed charges?

- Social implications: What are the social and religious stigmas, stereotypes, and stories associated with smoking weed? How have those narratives influenced the way I feel about marijuana use?

As activists working to free ourselves and others, we must consider the impacts of weed in our society and why so many people are in jail for possession while others legally grow it in their backyards and casually shop for their favorite strains of sativa or indica cannabis products at their local high-end dispensaries and CBD shops, which are now popular all over, especially in the suburbs.

In the United States, cannabis criminalization was designed to be political and racist, and it remains that way to this day. Those of us who consume weed, work in the cannabis industry, or benefit from the plant in any way have a responsibility to know its place in American history. Understanding how politicians and the government have used policies on marijuana to divide us is an important part of the fight to decriminalize weed as we strive for a legal and equitable future for everyone in the weed community, particularly Black people who have been targeted and have suffered greatly as a result of the war on drugs.

ARTIFACT

Three Acts That Weaponized Weed against Black Americans

(Find the reference for the full article listed in the bibliography.)

1. The Marihuana Tax Act of 1937

2. The Controlled Substances Act of 1970

3. The Violent Crime Control and Law Enforcement Act of 1994

FIFTY-EIGHT

Cannabis as Liberation

Getting high" is a term I am using to describe our ability to feel all things positive and free. When we get high, with weed or without weed, when we own our highest expression of our spiritual and sexual selves, that is when we pose the greatest threat to oppression. If we wish to get free, we've got to feel everything. We must know how good we can feel and decide not to run away from that. We've got to get high and get serious about it.

Not everyone experiences good sensations when they get high on marijuana. But for others, being high on marijuana induces a state of euphoria.

I got high for the first time at age forty-one. Before that, my feelings about weed were a manufactured and complicated mess, wrapped up in my religious upbringing and my childhood in California during Nancy Reagan's "Just Say No" era, filled with DARE program ads and the fried eggs in the "This is your brain on drugs, any questions?" commercial.

My first experience of getting high was a magical reenactment of the ancestral plane scene from the movie *Black Panther*, followed by what to me was some of the best sex I'd ever had with my wife. She, on the other hand, was having a totally different experience while being high and it was awful. She felt anxious and paranoid and saw me as a ninety-year-old woman during sex and she did not enjoy that at all.

I acknowledge and recognize those opposing experiences as I continue this discussion of my relationship with weed.

Because for me, getting high feels like stepping into some kind of heaven . . .

Dawn and I lived in Atlanta where weed wasn't legal, and it wasn't something that I had access to or sought to get. So for about a year or two, getting high wasn't something that I did very often, but in November 2019, a few weeks before we got the envelope in the door alerting us that our rental house was about to go into foreclosure, we decided to take a spontaneous trip to Denver, where weed was legal. There we found a local dispensary where I was introduced to the wide and wonderful world of weed. After I explained to the guy behind the counter that I was a newbie, he made some recommendations and we left with a brand-new vape pen and a little vial of some flavor-infused weed oil. I didn't love the taste, which was a bit chemical, but it certainly got the job done. I spent the next several days of our Colorado trip experimenting with how it felt to be high, a little high, a lot high. I observed myself as my state became altered slowly, how it felt on the climb up. I observed myself kind of floating around and feeling so very much in my body and out of it at the same time. I felt air going into my nose and I could follow the sensation as it traveled through my body and made every organ and cell it touched feel lighter and easier.

I loved the sensation. So when it came time for me to be intentional about going on hiatus, knowing the kind of feelings and sensations I wanted to tap into as much as possible, I left for California and then eventually Jamaica where I could have pretty much unrestricted access to all the weed I wanted.

That's why during the summer of 2020, I developed a real relationship with ganja.

In Jamaica, weed was plentiful, easily accessible, and super cheap after I went from buying weed at the local dispensary on the Hip Strip (the touristy area of Montego Bay where many of the shops, restaurants, and hotels line the street facing the Caribbean Sea) to rolling my own spliffs after about four months of practicing.

I spent every single day in some state of being high. In the beginning, I didn't have to consume very much to get there, but as the weeks and months went on, my tolerance increased, so I smoked more. One of the things I loved most of all about getting high was that there was no crash. Flying with the birds and the stars didn't conclude with falling down to earth where I would hurt myself as I used to after a night of drinking and doing shots in my thirties.

I stopped drinking alcohol in October 2019, the month before we went to Denver and I got immersed in the world of weed. I quickly discovered that no matter how high I got, I didn't experience any of the negative side effects, like the hangovers I used to get the day after getting drunk.

As I explored and observed myself smoking weed and being high, I banished my previous, uneducated misconceptions about the evils of weed. As I lived and moved around the island of Jamaica for almost a year, I saw firsthand that weed was literally just a plant, something that grew out of the ground, as natural as the sugarcane that the colonizers mined and raped the island for, using generations of Black labor stolen from Africa and taken to the Caribbean. Except for the Maroons, who resisted the colonizers and fled to the hills of Jamaica, refusing to be enslaved, who killed before allowing themselves to be captured and shackled. I was smoking the very plants that they had cultivated and smoked. Jamaican weed was the medicine of Black victory and Black liberation. It was a gift to me. And I received it daily.

FIFTY-NINE

Get High

When I got high, my inner voice became clearer, or maybe it was that my ears heard beyond the noise to the voices and sweet sounds of other spirits and ancestors and guides who I came to understand were always present with me. It was just a matter of whether I was in a state of consciousness where I could observe them. When I got high and meditated, I had access to all of them, to all of myself.

This is what I mean when I say "get high." Whether with the use of cannabis or without, there are many ways to experience this expansiveness. Weed is just one of those ways for me, and it was the first way I experienced this particular level of intensity in my spirituality through plant medicine.

As liberation activists who want to be free and help others get free as well, we need to consider that people smoke weed and get high for many different reasons. Many people use marijuana because it allows them to be more creative, and so it is popular among artists, musicians, and writers. For many whose lives are hard and complex, particularly people in poor and Black communities, smoking weed should be encouraged as a natural way to just feel good in their bodies and to feel relief, even a bit of an escape, from the effects of living in a cruel world.

Society conditions us to doubt and fear and mistrust what we feel. It is the patriarchy that is responsible for turning us against our own feelings, scaring us into believing that whatever feeling comes from weed is a bad feeling that will lead us to sin and to death.

We live in a society that doesn't want us to exist in the way that weed makes us feel, but wants instead to keep us drunk and violent on legal alcohol, numb and afraid on sermons from pulpits. Any society that wants to keep us from feeling good and prevents us from, warns us against, and punishes us for using natural substances and indigenous medicines that help us get into our bodies is a society committed to killing us, a society that would rather see us dead, which is why alcohol is not only legal but woven into the fabric of our culture, despite its devastating impacts on people, families, and communities.

Get fucking high. Find the thing that makes you feel this free; where you know thyself without question, without doubt, without fear. When you get carried away in the precious moment of now. That is the high of freedom and the high of living this life.

Whatever makes you come alive in that way, it is on that which you must get high.

Oppression has a feeling and that feeling is fear. Feeling good and getting high is a threat to oppression. When we feel good, when we feel energized, when we feel rested and take full belly breaths, we will know joy. Our liberation is wherever our joy lives. Whether in the US, Jamaica, Costa Rica, or wherever we are on the planet, we are liberated when we have full stomachs, full hearts, and deep, full breaths. Comfort is a feeling. Security is a feeling. Love is a feeling. Getting high is the feeling of getting free.

SIXTY

Draw Your Pleasure
Treasure Map

> The erotic is a measure between the beginnings of our sense of self and the chaos of our strongest feelings. It is an internal sense of satisfaction to which, once we have experienced it, we know we can aspire.
>
> —AUDRE LORDE, "USES OF THE EROTIC: THE EROTIC AS POWER"

Are we free yet . . . to get to the highs that draw the maps to our inner halls of treasures and pleasures?

Not everyone will choose the same paths toward healing. Not everyone has been called to plant medicines. It isn't about one way or one method. It is about opening yourself to receive the truest and lightest pathways that will guide you to your own healing and your own liberation. Your freedom song is known to you and no one else, and only you can write it. Your freedom path isn't going to look like the paths of those who came before you, and the freedom paths we draw for ourselves won't look like the paths of those who will come after us.

When anyone or anything tries to force you to follow their way of living and existing, that will lead you to more suffering and oppression. Free people write their own treasure and pleasure maps. Find the free people. Find the high people. Find the feeling people. The free, the high, the feeling people won't be telling you how to be, how to feel, or how to live your life. The free, high, feeling people will be celebrating all the ways you found to come home to yourself. The free ones will honor all your remarkable queerness. They will know to honor and respect and celebrate you as you journey to the freedom many have yet to discover.

JOURNAL PROMPT

With so many ways to tap into higher sensation and vibration, from body movement and physical activity to meditation to plant medicine and beyond, in what ways are you getting high? How does getting high operate in your liberation journey?

ARTIFACT
Weed Playlist

1. "Legalize It" performed by Peter Tosh

2. "A Vibe" performed by Protoje with Wiz Khalifa

3. "Kickin' Back" performed by Mila J

4. "Sativa" performed by Jhené Aiko with Swae Lee

5. "Roll Some Mo" performed by Lucky Daye

6. "Purple Haze" performed by Jimi Hendrix

7. "I Got 5 On It" performed by Luniz with Michael Marshall

8. "Stay High" performed by Brittany Howard

9. "Sober" performed by Childish Gambino

10. "Lighter" performed by Tarrus Riley with Shenseea and Rvssian

11. "Medication" performed by Damien Marley

12. "Peaches" performed by Justin Bieber, Usher, Snoop Dogg, Ludacris

SIXTY-ONE

Get into Your Body

> And O my people, out yonder, hear me, they do not love your neck unnoosed and straight. So love your neck; put a hand on it, grace it, stroke it and hold it up. And all your inside parts that they'd just as soon slop for hogs, you got to love them. The dark, dark liver—love it, love it, and the beat and beating heart, love that too. More than eyes or feet. More than lungs that have yet to draw free air. More than your life-holding womb and your life-giving private parts, hear me now, love your heart. For this is the prize.
>
> —TONI MORRISON

Our bodies deserve rest. Our bodies deserve restoration. Our bodies deserve to reclaim all that has been taken from us.

We must learn—or relearn—to trust the sensations of our bodies. All that we feel is part of our guidance system directing us toward living a full and free life. But as working and serving the community became perverted by exploitation and capitalism, we became detached from and desensitized to our bodies, increasingly reliant and dependent on our own oppression. We have been conditioned not to seek joy even though we have always had access to it. Joy is always there once we choose to experience it, deciding and demanding that all parts of our lives feel that way.

When we stay in toxic relationships—personal, political, or sexual—we sacrifice our bodies. As a result of capitalism, our physical bodies suffer invisible and covert blows that bruise our nonphysical being. But as we begin to heal on an internal level, we can start to get back into our bodies, where we can feel freedom. Our precious and remarkable bodies store so much inherent knowledge, so much ancestral wisdom, so much generational trauma, which makes our bodies a central location for our healing, a sacred space in which our liberating ceremonies take place.

Our bodies are our blessings, and we must care for them in the most intentional of ways. Connecting back to the wisdom inherent in our bones requires taking time to rid our minds of old lies about what our bodies should look like and how they should operate based on the dominant culture and its racist, sexist, anti-Black, fat-phobic, ableist social conditioning.

Reclaiming our sense of autonomy over our bodies gives us the power to fight for our bodies, which also gives us cause to celebrate them. How are we practicing for a revolution we haven't seen yet? Individually, there must be a personal revolution to reclaim our bodies. A lot of our love stories with ourselves grow out of war stories about our relationship with our bodies and how much pain and fear we have stored there. Being in our bodies involves forgiving ourselves for internalizing harmful messages about our physicality and our humanness.

Being in our bodies means doing things that take us out of our heads. Being in our bodies means being in the place beyond our thoughts where we tend to overthink and rationalize why we have to stay where we aren't wanted. Get in your body so you can listen closer and locate where you need to be and what you need in order to feel safe and be at home in your body. And where you need to celebrate.

SIXTY-TWO

Dance

Hard times require furious dancing.
—ALICE WALKER

Few things inspire and capture the beauty and resilience and joy of Blackness quite the way that dancing does. It was when I found myself able to dance again that I knew grief wasn't going to kill me. The more I danced, the more I felt like I was healing. When you find yourself able to dance, that is when you will feel in your bones that the grief isn't going to kill you. The more you dance, the more you will feel healing taking place in your body.

To those with physical limitations or disabilities, sexual trauma, body dysmorphia, or other physical challenges, I encourage you to explore ways to get into your body at the capacity that you are able.

SIXTY-THREE

Honor All the Parts of Yourself, Then and Now

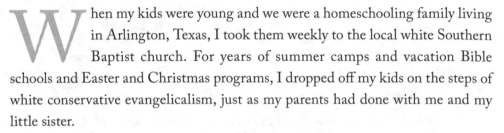

When my kids were young and we were a homeschooling family living in Arlington, Texas, I took them weekly to the local white Southern Baptist church. For years of summer camps and vacation Bible schools and Easter and Christmas programs, I dropped off my kids on the steps of white conservative evangelicalism, just as my parents had done with me and my little sister.

I easily rationalized that this was an important part of their needed "socialization" as homeschoolers. And as a worn-out stay-at-homeschooling mom, I appreciated the space it gave me, the reprieve from being around my kids 24/7, as well as the activities it provided to my poor family at no cost. We were always granted scholarships. For everything. All three of my kids. Very few to no questions asked. And if I'm being honest, times I spent with my kids at that church are some of the best memories I have of those years I homeschooled them.

I still fondly remember taking my daughters to the mother-daughter nights at that church, where we, along with dozens of primarily white moms and their white daughters, all dressed in matching pajamas. Together, all of us did arts and crafts, ate pizza, posed for professional photo shoots, and watched and danced along to every sequel of Disney's *High School Musical*.

Those were absolutely moments of mommy joy for me, even though in that environment we were the token Black family. I didn't interact with the adults much, but occasionally I volunteered to help chaperone on some of the overnight trips, so I could spend time with my kids and contribute to this church that was providing these activities to us for free. It seemed the least I could do. And I didn't hate it.

Reflecting back, I've asked myself: How could I have so easily participated in such religious oppression? Yes, my kids loved it, and yes, it gave me a break from my stressful role as full-time parent, caregiver, and homeschool teacher, but I knew what they were being taught from the biblical lesson plans, and I knew what they were learning from the experience of being Black kids in an all-white children's program at an all-white church, because that had been my childhood too.

I've made the decision to honor who I was then and give her grace, knowing that she did the best she could do. On our healing journeys, we must choose to respect the fact that we haven't always done things that we are proud of. We have to hold space for who we used to be and where we have come from, and honor our ability to reflect, change, and grow.

JOURNAL PROMPT

Which parts of the old you, or the transitioning you, do you need to forgive and honor?

SIXTY-FOUR

Forgiveness

L iberation invites us to consider and forgive who we used to be when we were still very much hidden, oppressed, and enslaved, and honor who we were then. Forgiveness is the process of releasing the harm and damage caused to us, either by ourselves or by others, and it is a self-love practice that we will engage in for the rest of our lives. The only way to reconcile the assimilated past versions of ourselves and the free humans we are becoming is by forgiving ourselves for what we had to do to survive. Unforgiveness breeds bitterness, resentment, and self-judgment that are counterproductive to our healing and our ability to move forward into lives of freedom.

A POEM ABOUT DUST

Dust is what gathers from what was or
    is present
Shoes that go walk around town
Return to the home with remnants of
    things
And bring with them dust
That if allowed settles somewhere
And dust always is
It's either in homes

Or on its way into homes
Or on its way out of homes
But even dust in the trash
Is still dust
It's just dust somewhere else
The reason we have to clean
Is that if we don't attend to it regularly
It will pile up and consume everything
There is energetic dust

And I want to get to a place where I
    am not collecting the old energetic
    residue
I want to get to a place where I am free
    because I have the choice
I don't have to hate everything that I
    used to be
And I don't have to hate America
This is clearing the dust
This is a way that I am honoring myself
Just because I am divorcing America
    doesn't mean I have to burn all our
    pictures
I still get to keep them on my phone
And go through them and smile and
    laugh in memory
Of how much fun
And how much joy
Belonged to those moments
And that version of me
And I don't have to cancel her
Or delete that memory
It gets to remain in my heart
If I so choose
That is the freedom
In the choice

It's up to me what I do with that dust
America is a racist white cis-het
    husband
Who is abusive
Physically
Emotionally
Spiritually
Financially
We've been in a relationship for as long
    as I can remember
And it has always been abusive
Even though sometimes it has also
    been happy
We have deep familial ties
That we somehow have managed to
    overlook when it suits us
I spent a few years planning to leave
Before finally leaving during the
    pandemic
For good
Then the world changed even though
    no one was waiting for it
I will listen
I will learn
I will love
I will change

SIXTY-FIVE

Rename Yourself

Allow me to reintroduce myself: my name is Lyontina. When my dad was in kindergarten, there was a girl in his class named Lyontina, and he decided then that when he grew up, he would give his daughter that name. Apparently, my mom was fine with that.

By the time I got to kindergarten at the predominantly white institution that was the Christian private school in Silicon Valley I attended through sixth grade, I was already tired of my name that few people could pronounce correctly. Even my Creole grandparents didn't say it right. Though the way they called me "Luntina" felt warm, that was not the case with white teachers, who, despite correction, never made it a point to consistently say my name correctly. By the time I was in middle school, I went by Tina.

When I got pregnant with Chelsea, Chaz wanted to name her Khadijah. After all, it was 1996, and Khadijah was the name of the character played by Queen Latifah in the Black young adult sitcom *Living Single*. Despite his request, I named her Chelsea instead. But after she was born, Chaz remembered something that he had completely forgotten about: when he was a kid and played peewee football back in Bear Creek in Irving, Texas, one of his teammates had a sister named Chelsea and Chaz had decided that when he grew up, he would name his daughter Chelsea. He remembered this only when he was holding our new baby girl, Chelsea, in his hands, just days before he shipped out to South Korea to serve a year of his tour of duty as a soldier in the US Army.

Chazare and Lyontina's baby girl made an incredible comeback after her mental health crisis in May 2020. She entered law school at Berkeley in the fall of 2022, and one day, her name, Chelsea Strawn, will ring in the halls of justice.

I've had to find and extend a lot of grace for Lyontina, and for the decision I made to stop using my given name because people couldn't pronounce it.

When we get married, the patriarchal tradition is for the woman to take on her husband's name. There is ceremony and celebration attached to naming; there is sacredness involved when we name the children we bring into this world. Let there be celebration in reclaiming and renaming.

My grandma renamed herself. She was born Mattie, but in her adulthood, she chose to go only by Olivia, which was her middle name . . . which is also my middle name and why I selected Olivia as my name for "Honoring the Ori," the article included earlier. Because Olivia was what my grandmother chose to name herself, who she chose to be.

As descendants of African slaves, we must rename ourselves. Our names were lost, left on West African shores, drowned in deep waters that carried boats with beings below to lands that could not hold peace for slave trades. As beautiful and blessed bodies were bought and sold, names were assigned by masters who claimed ownership over flesh, blood, and bones that were never meant to be owned. Shackles were placed on those who were forced to bear the names of those whom the shackles belonged to. But what is the name of the shackle remover? What shall they call you now?

Your name carries the memories. Can you go to free land bearing the name of your enslaver? Can you remain free when you continue to answer to the name your enslaver used to summon you?

Gift yourself your free name.

JOURNAL PROMPT

What would you have yourself be named? What do you want to be called? Does your slave name feel true? Does it ring in your ears as what your soul answers to?

SIXTY-SIX

Be Gracious

According to *The Four Agreements*, a book by the spiritual teacher Don Miguel Ruiz, we're not supposed to take shit personal. That was the hardest part for me to process when it came to Dawn leaving me, texting me that she wanted a divorce, and then texting me eight months later to say that our divorce was final. To this day I have never seen or signed any divorce papers. The only reason I know I am divorced is that she texted me saying so.

To be honest, it has been only through this process toward my own liberation that I have learned what it means not to take things personally. Walking in grace and love for myself has led me to the place where I am learning to accept that my wife leaving was not about me. I'm learning about the healing and liberating power of being full of grace. First with myself, then with others.

I no longer take it personally when others don't like or love me. I only take it personal when I don't like or love me. I am not supposed to take America's hate for my queer, Black, woman body personal. And the more I liked and loved and valued myself and my Black life, the less I was willing to tolerate. The more I recognized my worth and that I was meant to live with full dignity and freedom, the more I realized it was time for me to go.

Extend grace to yourself first, in whatever ways you choose to leave and in whatever ways you choose to stay.

SIXTY-SEVEN

Find Restorative
"Poetic" Justice

restorative justice (noun): a justice framework wherein the consenting person(s) harmed and the person(s) who caused the harm participate in a process of repair that centers the person(s) harmed and seeks to restore them to their original state, while also addressing the systemic and structural factors that caused and allowed the harm to happen in the first place.

Restorative justice is done in a community environment and context and involves acknowledgment, apology, and affirmation on the part of the offender to stop causing the harm and to take accountability for finding ways to restore the person harmed to their original state; the process also seeks to address the underlying social or environmental factors at the root of the harm. I am calling it "poetic" as our invitation as individuals is to take a restorative justice approach in how we interact and engage with our friends and loved ones and others in our communities. An example of restorative justice would be the return of wealth to Black Americans by the US government through reparations. An example of restorative poetic justice would be participation by ex-partners in an uncoupling ceremony after a breakup.

Restorative justice is the abolitionist response and is the opposite of punitive justice. It doesn't throw anyone away, no matter the harm, offense, or damage. And it goes beyond the simple apology to giving the harmed person(s) the ability to use their voice and name what they need to feel and be restored.

For activists who are love- and justice-focused, there must be space between spouses, friends, even in our romantic and intimate relationships, where we can imagine and create a way that when conflict arises, no one is thrown away. We must imagine ways that we can work through changes and shifts in relationships where we're not just destroying people, their hearts, or their lives.

It does us no good to have this grand concept of liberty if we can't figure out how to move differently in our interpersonal relationships. Breakups and conflict happen. People change and grow apart and people sometimes choose to part and go their separate ways. Reparations, repair, restoration, and abolition must become critical components of our personal and political value system of liberation. This is what we must write in our contracts when we commit to getting free together.

Liberation activists, like abolitionists, must be the kind of free people who don't make a mess of everything and then walk away with hands thrown up in the air. That's what whiteness does (see again: slavery). We must be the ones who demonstrate how to repair the harm that we cause, and our ability to challenge ourselves to practice this radical style of restorative justice, even in our personal lives, can be poetic.

Justice needs to take place in our homes to reflect the dreams we hold in our hearts of the kind of world we want to live in. That's what being a liberation activist means, practicing how we live out and live through what we want to see, and who we want to be in the world.

SIXTY-EIGHT

Queer Black Sheep

I have never wanted to look too deeply into African traditional religions because I feared I would just find the same rejection and patriarchal judgment in them that I found in the evangelical Christian church that raised me. I have already had the experience of both white and Black Jesus condemning me to a fiery hell for all eternity for being gay, so I am uninterested in discovering more religious doctrines and elders and teachers beyond the veil and from the motherland who curse me like conservative Christians and their savior did.

As a queer woman born into a "proper" family, I am this queer Black sheep who has the ability to love and be attracted to people regardless of gender. It doesn't feel complicated for me anymore like it used to when I was trying to fit my queer self into the proper boxes. It feels beautiful. There's no restriction on who I can love and who I desire and who I want to be in a relationship with. Being queer feels like the biggest blessing. It is a gift. I have a bias toward being queer. I feel bad for cis-het people because all they get is one gender. As my spiritual life became deeper and richer over the years following my coming out, I had a strong secret wish to receive some affirmation, a blessing, from Spirit.

As I was sitting down one day and working on this book, the ancestors answered my heart's inquiry in a powerful way. I was writing about some of the tools of healing, such as spiritual practices, breathing, meditation, and mindfulness, when my attention was brought directly to a specific part of "Honoring the Ori," the article about my experience working with Dr. Candice and her team, that I had totally forgotten about.

On the first day of my intensive therapy retreat, when we began our meditation session, one of my therapists did an ancestral ritual. As we were still and focused on our breathing, she specifically asked for any words that my ancestors had for me. My ancestors came through. They came through with a message to tell me to keep going . . . *and they blessed me.*

It has taken me many years to shed the fear of the curses and eternal damnation with which I was threatened and indoctrinated. So a key aspect to my getting free has been receiving queer blessings. And an aspect of my joy and celebration practice is knowing that one day, I will be a queer ancestor who will bless queer generations that come after me.

ARTIFACT
Queer Morning Blessings

By Dori Midnight and Randy Furash-Stewart

(caress your eyes)
Blessed are you, AWAKENER, life of all worlds, who removes sleep from my eyes and slumber from my eyelids.

(feel your feet upon the solid ground)
Blessed are you, GENEROUS CREATRIX, who stretches forth the earth upon the waters.

(receive light, take in your surroundings)
Blessed are you, SACRED FLAME, who illuminates and shines upon everyone and everything.

(dust off your shoulders, run your hands across your limbs, touch the fabrics touching you)
Blessed are you, HOLY FASHION DESIGNER, who delights in the way we dress ourselves as altars.

(move from tightness to stretching wide)
Blessed are you, LIBERATION WORKER, who moves us to stretch and expand towards freedom.

(feel yourself)
Blessed are you, DIVINE APPLE ORCHARD, who delights in my delight and is praised by my pleasure.

(touch your heart)
Blessed are you, NAMELESS AND INFINITE, who made us in your image and reminds us that all bodies are sacred and holy.

(place a crown upon your head and lift your chin)
Blessed are you, WINGS OF GOLD, who crowns my people, all people, with splendor.

(take a breath that fills your whole body, hold it for a moment, and let it out)
Blessed are you, HOLY BREATH, who fills me with this gift every day.

(open your palms in front of you)
Blessed are you, ABUNDANCE, who helps me remember I have everything I need.

(let your body move as it wants to move)
Blessed are you, THE WAY, who meets me where I am.

(close your eyes and rest)
Blessed are you, SOURCE OF LIFE, who I draw on for strength and who reminds me that rest is a sacred act.

(embrace yourself)
Blessed are you, FABULOUS ONE, who loves me just as I am.

(place your hand somewhere that needs extra love)
Blessed are you, WEAVER OF BEING, who shaped the human being with wisdom, making for us all the openings and vessels of the body. It is known that we are miracles and all bodies are miracles.

Blessed are you, YOU OF MANY NAMES, for revealing infinite paths of healing.

SIXTY-NINE

Follow Your Joy

> Once we recognize what it is we are feeling, once we recognize we can feel deeply, love deeply, can feel joy, then we will demand that all parts of our lives produce that kind of joy.
>
> —AUDRE LORDE

Getting free has everything to do with following our joy. It is joy that must become our guide to living a liberated life. When joy shows up in your life, welcome and embrace it. And then start to expect it. Become a student of joy.

An effect of oppression is that we carry a lot of baggage and shame around experiencing pleasure and joy. We tend to limit how much joy we allow ourselves to feel. Our capitalist society benefits when joy is just beyond our reach, when joy is something that we think we must strive for. For example, play for the sake of playing isn't encouraged, but rather we are conditioned to use play and joy as rewards for hard work. When we reserve joy only for when we feel we deserve it, then we also justify the lack of joy in our lives as punishment for not working hard enough.

Living a life of joy takes a lot of courage. Following our joy is the opposite of living in fear, and that is scary and intimidating for many people. We must be intentional about noticing and recognizing our moments of joy so we can expand them into our way of life.

It is my belief that when we follow our joy, the odds, and the risks, are ever in our favor.

SEVENTY

My Solo Poly Honeymoon

Freeing yourself was one thing; claiming ownership of that free self was
another.

—TONI MORRISON

A new friend that I made in Jamaica, a fellow Black woman from the States
also escaping to the island for sunshine and peace, invited me to join her
at an all-inclusive resort in Trelawny, not far from where I was living in
Montego Bay. I decided to check in and stay for a few days as a treat to myself. I
declared it my solo poly honeymoon.

Having been forced to accept my new reality as a future ex-wife for the second
time, I resigned myself to letting go and committed to crafting a relationship path
of my choosing, one more suited to where I saw myself heading, full of joy, celebration, and radical self-love. I had started looking into the world of polyamory.
One of the things that immediately appealed to me was that its very definition—
having multiple loving relationships at the same time from an ethical nonmonogamous standpoint—sounded so natural and communal to me. Community was
something that I wanted more of in my life, in a revolutionary "it takes a village"
kind of way. As a mother of three children, I understood very clearly what it was
to love multiple humans fully, simultaneously, and equally, yet differently.

But parenting and marriage are completely different things. In a world where
we are surrounded by cis-heteronormative expectations that value monogamous
marriage as the highest relationship one can attain, I had never even heard of

polyamory in a true sense until my early forties. I had certainly not seen an example of this alternative relationship type. So I had no concept of what being poly really looked like in everyday life and love.

But since my wife and I had been living in our marriage over the past few years with very little sex, I began to warm up to the idea that it is not possible for one person, our spouse, to meet all our needs. And that expectation is injustice.

I remembered how, earlier in the year, right before we moved out of our Little Elm house, I had lain awake in bed one night, soft thoughts and prayers rolling around in my head, thinking that I wanted more. I knew without question that I loved my wife, but I wanted to follow that fact to a deeper truth . . . I loved my wife so much that I wanted a fulfilling sex life for her, even if it meant with someone else. And for whatever reason, that didn't feel like such an odd desire. It actually felt good thinking about my wife getting completely satisfied and filled sexually by another woman. It made for remarkable fantasies too. So it was settled. In my mind. I wanted amazing sex lives for myself and for my wife, even if that meant both of us having other sexual partners. After we were separated and both of us had discovered great sex with new people, I started looking into poly more.

Though unskilled and inexperienced in any relationship style other than monogamy, having spent a total of almost eighteen years as a wife to both a husband of eleven years and a wife of seven years, I was eager to find what I hoped would look and feel like freedom in my new acceptance of an ethically nonmonogamous life.

Ethical nonmonogamy described how I had been engaging with my sexual partners since my wife and I had been separated. Polyamory described a new way to be in relationship with multiple people at once. During my research into abundant loving (another term I use to describe poly), I was introduced to solo polyamory and adopted this term for myself to mean that I would be my own primary partner, and whether or not I chose to have additional partners, my relationship with myself would come first and foremost, above all others, both in theory and in practice.

It only made sense to seal this decision to become solo poly with a celebration.

My choice to be solo poly was so intentional that I began using my own behaviors as a wife as a template to show love and affection toward myself. After all, loving my spouses (particularly a husband) was what I had been preparing for since I was a little girl playing house with my baby dolls and Barbies, since the church indoctrination of my youth when I made celibacy promises to present my virginity to my husband as a gift of my purity and unwavering and undying love to him and only him. I was an exceptional child bride type, a wife wannabe. And I turned into a hopeful if less-than-exceptional wife in real life. Taking care of the needs and anticipating the wants of my spouses came more naturally to me (due to socialization and conditioning) than taking care of and anticipating my own wants and needs.

This became my solo poly map: if it was something that I wouldn't hesitate to do in my marriages to my spouses, then I would consciously choose not to hesitate to do that thing in my relationship with myself. I decided that I would court myself, date myself, spoil myself . . . "spoiling" always being a term that I had mixed feelings about, understanding that many used it in a negative way, but I always saw "spoiled" as meaning well taken care of, and that wasn't something that I wanted to disassociate myself from. As I looked back on my marriages, I saw that I had been loved and I had been well taken care of, in so many ways. I also loved my spouses well and knew how to "spoil" them. In turn, I would set out to spoil myself.

This was the new way of life and of love and of justice for myself. I had been through a hellish year and I was coming out on the other side holding my own hand and declaring myself home with this week-long proposal, acceptance, marriage, celebration, and declaration of love to my own damn self. It felt wicked. It felt decadent. It felt indulgent. It felt joyful.

I wondered how my view of myself would have been different had I started on this path toward loving myself this way sooner. Without judging my experience of mothering and wifing and granting myself and my own parents a tremendous measure of grace, I know that I did the best that I could to take care of myself and those I was entrusted to love: my children, my husband, and my wife. I wondered if my view of myself and my relationship with myself would have made a difference to my three children as they were growing up. My questions of "Is it too late?" sprung from a maternal desire to demonstrate that I wanted them to live their best lives and choose a life that they loved purposefully every day, starting with the love they had for themselves. I didn't teach them that when they were growing up because no one taught that to me. I hope that though my season of parenting them has shifted now that my nest is empty and they are flying on their own, they can still see and learn that being in love and in relationship with others is important and beautiful, but not at the expense of losing ourselves.

SEVENTY-ONE

The Pleasure and Politics of Polyamory

The last time I had seen them was outside a Hilton Hotel in the business district of downtown San Francisco. He was catching an Uber to his soccer game as he kissed his wife goodbye. And then, to my surprise, he turned and kissed me goodbye too. An actual, brief but full-on kiss on the lips. The sensation of surprise and pleasure spread through my body at this unexpected gesture. His wife, standing next to me, just smiled as we both waved him off. This felt sweet and tender in a way that I knew I wanted more of in my life, in my heart, and in my bed where the three of us, the couple and I, had just spent hours on that glorious Sunday morning and into the afternoon, only a few days after we'd met on the threesome app and had our very first sexual encounter.

This love, theirs and ours, was no ordinary love.

Apparently, they wanted more of that kind of love too. Because a few months later, they accepted my invitation to come visit me in Jamaica for a week.

Over that week, I got to observe myself in the presence of this loving couple. Our time together was beautiful, as passionate as it was purposeful. For me, that week was less about the sex and more about what I could learn about ethical nonmonogamy and polyamory through this firsthand experience.

From the outside, I was sharing moments of intimacy with both of them, separately and together. But on the inside, I was examining what it could mean for me to open up my heart, mind, and perspective around consensual romantic and intimate relationships with more than one person.

This felt like a future kind of love that I had the privilege and the honor of witnessing and participating in. I became a student of possibility, learning what it was like to love both a man and a woman at the same time. They helped me to see that my capacity for pleasure wasn't something I should try to restrict or tame at all. They taught me that fantasy can be a sweet reality. With them, my queerness got to be fully expressed and unapologetically celebrated. I never knew I could want this, let alone have it. I didn't know it was possible for me to enjoy two humans in this way simultaneously, without the confines and restrictions of gender roles or the rigid relationship rules and expectations that I had been used to my whole life. What was this new joy I had found between these two loving people and me?

I moved forward from my queerest week of the year committed to exploring, learning about, and practicing ethical nonmonogamy and polyamory as my chosen relationship style.

The activist in me wanted to move my examination and exploration of polyamory from the personal to the political. That exploration has led me to a path of questioning and confronting how monogamy and the institution of marriage itself function in a society built on white supremacy, capitalism, and the patriarchy. I have learned about the history of monogamy and the institution of marriage, the way society privileges married people over unmarried people (in everything from tax benefits to health insurance coverage), the history behind why women take their husband's last name, how single and/or divorced women are treated socially and religiously, and so much more. And like any marriage, and also like any divorce, I expect that this study I have embarked on will be wide and deep and full of new information and adventure.

The takeaway for people seeking all forms of liberation is to let your fantasies feed your curiosities. And then let your curiosities transform your realities. We have the ability and the power to experience so much more if we open our hearts and our minds. This is the queer way, the joy-centered way . . . to push back on and ultimately remove restrictions and barriers that were put in place by, and that uphold, systems of oppression . . . and to bust open the doors of expansion, inclusivity, belonging (not ownership), and liberation.

SEVENTY-TWO

Take Risks

So what is everyone afraid of, and what keeps us coloring inside fear-based lines? Being queer in a hetero-centric world taught me to take risks. And being queer continues to lead me to more boundaries and battle lines drawn in the homogeneous sand that I can dance over.

A POEM ABOUT RISK

I am a solo traveler
A woman solo traveler
A Black woman solo traveler
A queer Black woman solo traveler
I know I'm at risk
I know I'm at risk whether I'm moving
   or still
Whether I'm in my home country or
   abroad
Whether I sleep or rise
Whether I come or go
Or stay or leave
Whether I am sick or well
I am at risk
At risk of danger
And at risk of falling in love

At risk of being seen and seeing
   others
At risk of being followed and tracked
At risk of being waited for and
   waited on
At risk of loneliness
And of overstimulation
At risk of war and peace
Within and without
If I stay closed
I can't let anyone in
If I stay open
The love can flow
So I take the risk
And I follow the joy
You see I've been at risk since birth

My Black American mother was at risk
   when she birthed her queer Black
   American baby
Into a hostile world
But she carried me from her mother's
   womb
And her mother's womb
And hers
To here
So to think I was almost not here
To risk being born a queer Black
   woman
Among mortals
That is the true risk
I could have been born not Black, or
   not queer
And that would have been a tragedy
   to me
Time stands still while we stand here
Those were the first words, the line,
   the verse
I wanted to cum and attend to me this
   morning

As the incense pours its blessings
   on me
On this morning after
Being high with them, being in my
   body where everything is
   illuminated
While I lay there in the early hours
My fingers found their way to my portal
And this is what came to me
Touch is empowering
Liberating
Inspiring
Spirituality is everything
Sexuality is everything
We unlock so much of ourselves when
   we invite ourselves to step inside
   both truths
This is what I have set out to find
Where can a queer Black
   woman-identified human feel safe
   and find home
This is what I have set out to be
A free, queer, Black, joyful human

SEVENTY-THREE

Create Your Own Constitution of Joy

We the People of the United States, in Order to form a more perfect Union, establish Justice, insure domestic Tranquility, provide for the common defence, promote the general Welfare, and secure the Blessings of Liberty to ourselves and our Posterity, do ordain and establish this Constitution for the United States of America.

—PREAMBLE TO THE UNITED STATES CONSTITUTION

As people abandoned, forgotten, disregarded, and disrespected by the United States, we must ask ourselves if the founding documents that established this country actually provide freedom for all of us. To get free, I encourage you to write your own constitution of joy. Write a document setting yourself free, write a constitution of joy that you will sign with your new name, write a constitution of joy over which our ancestors will rejoice.

Use this template for creating your personal constitution of joy:

- Sing: Write your own freedom song or select one or a few from the playlists provided in this book.

- Eat: What recipes or rituals involving food can you include in your constitution of joy?

- Smoke: What are the ways you get high?

- Dance: What is a joy practice you will engage in that celebrates your body?

- Bless: Write a blessing over yourself and over your constitution of joy. If you choose to rename yourself, use your new, free name in this blessing.

  My hope for you, for me, and for all of us seeking to get free:

  > I hope you find some unreasonable joy.
  > I hope you rent luxury apartments on the beach.
  > I hope you get on Zoom calls and FaceTime with friends and loved ones for the purpose of celebrating yourself and celebrating one another.
  > I hope you create your own space to breathe.
  > I hope you acknowledge the ways you show up to heal and comfort yourself.
  > I hope you are gracious with yourself.
  > I hope you give yourself permission to love again.
  > I hope you watch sunrises and sunsets.
  > I hope you sing and dance.
  > I hope that amid so much Black death and loss you realize what a blessing it is to have/hold/honor this magical Black life that matters so much.
  > These are the things I commit to doing for us, for you and for me . . .
  > Until freedom rings.

JOURNAL PROMPT

How will you form a more perfect union for and with yourself? How will you allow grace and compassion with yourself to increase your capacity for living a life of joy?

* * *

ARTIFACT

AWFY Joy and Celebration Playlist

1. "UMI Says" performed by Mos Def

2. "Martin Was a Man, a Real Man" performed by Oliver Nelson Orchestra

3. "Black Superhero" performed by Robert Glasper, Killer Mike, BJ The Chicago Kid, Big K.R.I.T.

4. "Don't Touch My Hair" performed by Solange, Sampha

5. "Alright" performed by Kendrick Lamar

6. "This Is America" performed by Childish Gambino

7. "Scream" performed by Michael Jackson, Janet Jackson

8. "Where I'm Coming From" performed by Lila Iké

9. "What's Going On" performed by Marvin Gaye

10. "River" performed by Ibeyi

11. "I Can't Breathe" performed by H.E.R.

12. "Django Jane" performed by Janelle Monae

PART

IV

Activism *and* Liberation

SEVENTY-FOUR

The Case for Divorcing America

The most disrespected person in America is the Black woman. The most unprotected person in America is the Black woman. The most neglected person in America is the Black woman.

—MALCOLM X

No one goes into marriage thinking they are going to get divorced. "Until death do us part"—that's the language we use. We say our vows and mean them with all our hearts, until we don't. Likewise, most of us have spent our lives placing hands over hearts and reciting, "I pledge allegiance to the flag of the United States of America . . ."

Until the time came for us to take a knee during the national anthem instead.

Living through racial terror and violence, disappointment, broken promises, disrespect, neglect, and abuse, we can't help but question those vows. Am I really going to stay in this abusive and toxic relationship until I die? After two divorces, I have become very clear on what it looks like to end a marriage and all the doubt and questioning that takes place: How can I afford to leave? Am I sure we can't work it out? Have I tried and done everything I could before walking out the door?

For me, I had arrived at a place with America where I said, "I just can't do this anymore."

SEVENTY-FIVE

Meeting Stacey Abrams

During my political activism days in September 2017, I was invited to listen to a Black woman who had just announced that she was running for governor of Georgia. There were only about fifty of us in a small meeting room at a local community center in a suburb of Atlanta. I remember noticing her passion and charisma and listening as she spoke so lovingly about her parents and about growing up Black and poor and in the church. She had been a tax attorney and an author who wrote romance novels using the pen name Selena Montgomery. She had a good reputation serving in the Georgia House of Representatives from 2007 to 2017, serving as minority leader from 2011 to 2017. She talked about the shame of having to file for bankruptcy because she had taken on the responsibility of helping to financially support her parents and siblings (including an incarcerated brother) and because she was drowning in six figures of student loan debt, a point that Georgia Republicans tried to use to show that she was irresponsible and unfit to be governor.

Abrams's primary focus was voting rights. And it was that night when I went to see and hear and take a picture with her, sweaty from rushing over after teaching a cycle class, that listening to her bold expressions of hope for what Georgia could be made me want to do all I could to support her in ways I had never supported a political candidate before. After learning what I did about voter suppression from Stacey Abrams, I became an official poll watcher for the Georgia Democrats and volunteered at numerous polling locations during the 2018 midterm season. As a poll watcher, I was responsible for observing and ensuring voting integrity at the polling place. Poll watching is a bipartisan role, but each party is responsible for providing its own poll watchers. We were not to interrupt the voting process; we were simply there to ensure that people who showed up to vote were allowed to do so without interference.

During the primary for the Democratic governor nomination, Stacey Abrams was up against Stacey Evans, so we watched as Georgia Democrats made a decision to throw support to white Stacey or Black Stacey, or as the media called it, "the battle of the Staceys."

After Abrams won the primary, she faced then secretary of state Brian Kemp.

It hadn't even occurred to me to wonder whether she was married or had kids, but I was quickly reminded of where I lived in relation to the Southern patriarchy because Kemp and the Republicans were always emphasizing how much of a family man Kemp was with his dutiful wife and kids, and sounding the age-old conservative dog whistle of "family values." As the acting secretary of state, whose function it was to oversee and supervise the elections, Kemp remained in this position and was responsible for the voting process and the outcome of the election that he himself was running in for governor. Meanwhile, Abrams gave up her seat in the Georgia House of Representatives during her gubernatorial campaign.

Between 2012 and 2018, Kemp's secretary of state office canceled over 1.4 million voter registrations, with nearly 700,000 cancellations in 2017 alone. On a single night in July 2017, half a million voter registrations were purged. Emory University scholar Carol Anderson has criticized Kemp as an "enemy of democracy" and "an expert on voter suppression" for his actions as secretary of state.

Not surprisingly, Kemp would ultimately steal the gubernatorial election that year.

On November 6, 2018, Abrams "lost" the election by 54,723 votes. Over the next ten days, I was on the team of volunteers who chased ballots to try to find votes that still needed to be counted, from absentee ballots to provisional ballots. On November 16, Abrams announced that she was ending her campaign. She emphasized that her statement was not a concession, because "concession means to acknowledge an action is right, true, or proper," but she recognized that she could not close the gap with Kemp to force a runoff. In her campaign-ending speech, Abrams announced the creation of Fair Fight Action, a nonprofit voting organization that would go on to sue Brian Kemp, the secretary of state who named himself governor, and the state election board in federal court for voter suppression.

SEVENTY-SIX

Evaluate Your Relationship
with the Democratic Party

F ast-forward to 2020, and Stacey Abrams was being considered to be the VP running mate to Democratic presidential candidate Joe Biden. It can easily be argued that a reason the Democratic Party selected California senator Kamala Harris over Abrams is that she was just the right amount of diversity needed to pacify the progressives without pissing off the moderates (too much). Harris checked so many DEI (Diversity, Equity, and Inclusion) boxes as a Black and South Asian woman with a white Jewish husband. The optics suggest that the Democratic Party and the nation weren't ready to receive a dark-skinned, natural-haired, husbandless and childless Black woman in a bigger body to serve in the second-highest government office in the land. The Democrats had the opportunity to choose Stacey Abrams but they didn't because she didn't fit into their brand.

As an activist and expat, I continue to see voting, or rather the concept of voting, as a very important civic duty. However, when it came time to vote for president of the United States in November 2020, I was not a fan of Biden or Harris so I remained conflicted about whether and how to use my absentee vote as a registered voter of DeKalb County, Georgia, while living in Montego Bay, Jamaica. On Election Day, I went to the local DHL shipping office and filled out the absentee ballot that I had received and sent my ballot in through rushed delivery, reluctantly casting my vote against Donald J. Trump. But it turned out that my ballot did not arrive in time to be counted. Joe Biden won anyway.

To vote Democrat just because they are not Republican is a tired, outdated strategy. To vote Democrat no matter how problematic the candidate is, how pro-police they are, how pro-capitalism they are, how anti-Black they are, is to be a slave to the Democratic Party and to disrespect oursleves and our ancestors and what they fought for. This is the consistent critique that Black feminists in partic-ular have been voicing for decades. The Democrats have repeatedly demonstrated that they can't and won't save us. We must save ourselves by looking to the myriad of ways that Black folx have been getting ourselves free for generations, and the most radical ways happen outside of all parties of whiteness.

JOURNAL PROMPT

In what ways do you think the Democratic Party has supported or abandoned Black vot-ers? What is the deal breaker for you in your relationship with the Democratic Party? Over which policies and broken promises are you willing to walk away from them?

SEVENTY-SEVEN

To Vote or Not to Vote

During the 2018 midterm election season, I personally hosted over a dozen voter registration drives around the Atlanta area. One of those drives was in the West End of Atlanta, an area that is widely considered to be the hood. One afternoon while getting my locs retwisted, I asked my loctician if she knew that there was a Black woman running for governor. She did not know this. In my circles everybody knew, so I couldn't imagine that anyone, let alone Black people, didn't know they had the opportunity to vote for a Black female governor during this historic election. I told her that I would love to get the word out about Abrams. I asked the shop owner if I could leave a Stacey Abrams campaign poster in the shop, and he said yes. I asked if I could come back and do a voter registration drive, to which he also said yes.

Two weeks later, I was there with my table and a few volunteers and we were talking to people as they walked by. I will never forget going up to an older Black gentleman who was wearing an African-print shirt.

"Excuse me, sir, are you registered to vote?" I asked happily.

He said no. I offered to register him so he could vote for the first Black woman governor in the United States. He looked me in the eyes and firmly explained why he wasn't voting.

"Vote?" he asked. "No, I'm not going to vote! I work every day to burn this system down." And he continued by saying, "Sista, you shouldn't be out here doing

this. This system is not for us. You should be out here with me, working to dismantle it."

At first, his words didn't make sense to me . . . wasn't voting the best way to
honor our ancestors who fought and died for our right to vote? That's what the
Democrats had always told us. But I couldn't ignore the feeling that it was one of
the most pro-Black and radical things I had ever heard.

Because what he was saying is what many Black feminists have been saying for
decades, and what Keeanga-Yamahtta Taylor describes in her introduction to the
book *How We Get Free*. It would take me a few years to fully understand and embrace that not voting can be a radical strategy toward liberation.

Here's the thing, not voting is still voting. Just as silence is an answer. As Black
women in particular, when we vote, our impact is felt. We win elections. The
modern-day Democratic Party knows and readily admits that its strongest group
of voters is Black women. And just as we win elections with our vote, the impact
of the absence of our Black women votes will be felt.

Why is it considered controversial to say that we should be voting only for candidates who earn our votes, and to threaten to take our votes away from candidates,
and political parties, who do not represent the people?

Black voters have been brainwashed to think that we must vote Democrat, every
time, no matter what, regardless of the candidate, the platform, and the principles
to which they subscribe. But here's the problem with that: voting Democrat does
not equate with voting for the best interests of the Black community or any other
marginalized community, in and of itself.

There is no disputing that our votes are valuable, which is why the Republicans
work very hard and are committed to suppressing the Black vote. However, we
must consider in what ways the political system is simply another vehicle for oppressive structures to be maintained and thrive—offering us only two choices,
Democrat or Republican. If we keep participating in the binary, then we are only
strengthening it. The fact is that the current voting system in this nation, with two
parties and an antiquated electoral college, is not broken. It is working exactly as
it was designed to work. At what point should we stop participating in it and burn
it down?

ACTIVITY

Learn about these third/alternative party options and seek out others: The Working Families Party, The Poor People's Campaign, The Green Party.

AWFY PRO TIP

- Get involved politically at the state and local levels to affect change where you live.

- Attend school board and city council meetings and support and engage with your local representatives and elected officials.

- Vote for candidates who share your racial and social justice values. Do not vote for candidates who do not share your racial and social justice values. Remove "Vote Blue No Matter Who" from your practice.

SEVENTY-EIGHT

Losing the Black Woman's Vote

In my work as a volunteer for the Abrams campaign as well as the campaign of a local Black woman, Essence Johnson, who was running for the Georgia House of Representatives seat for District 45 in 2018, it was all that I experienced and observed of how the local, state, and national Democratic Party treated Black women candidates that led me to leave the traditional political scene and go into antiracism education instead.

For those who believe that voting is one of the most important actions that can be taken to effect change in our nation, I implore you to carefully consider the voting trends of Black people, Black women in particular. Black people have historically been abandoned by the Democratic Party. And it is for this reason that the number of Black women voters has steadily declined and will continue to do so.

After watching Biden's March 2022 State of the Union address, and having experienced so much disappointment and many broken promises from the Biden administration—from his continued deportation of Black and Brown immigrants to his refusal to cancel student loan debt, to his admission of being a capitalist and his desire to increase police funding and so much more—I am grateful that my voting record does not show I ever voted for that man. And if Biden becomes the 2024 Democratic candidate, running against Trump or whomever the Republicans put up, I will not be bullied by the manipulative Democratic Party narrative that "not voting for Biden is a vote for Trump." I will not vote for Joseph Robinette Biden Jr. I will just be joining the millions of Black women who feel the same way.

Here is an excerpt from Keeanga-Yamahtta Taylor's introduction to the book *How We Get Free: Black Feminism and the Combahee River Collective*:

In the days after the disastrous 2016 presidential election, a popular meme showing that 94 percent of Black women voters had cast their ballot for Hillary Clinton was circulated as proof that Black women had done their part to keep Trump out of the White House. The meme, though, was misleading. It was true that 94 percent of Black women who voted cast their ballot for Clinton, but those voters represented 64 percent of all eligible Black women. Even though this was a large voter turnout, it represented a 6 percent drop in Black women's historically high turnout in 2012, when Barack Obama was on the ballot. Indeed, the overall turnout for Black voters declined for the first time in a presidential election in twenty years, falling to 59 percent from its historic high of 66 percent in 2012.

The search for answers to how the loathsome Donald J. Trump could become president of the United States tended to focus on who did and did not vote. Of course, that was part of the explanation, but what was often missing was closer scrutiny of what kept tens of millions of people from participating in the election. To that point, given Trump's repeated appeals to racism, why would fewer, not more, African Americans, including Black women, have participated in that critical election?

Any cursory investigation into the lives of African Americans would have revealed deep dissatisfaction with their conditions—even after the historic election of Barack Obama in 2008. After all, the last few years of the Obama presidency had seen the rise of the Black Lives Matter movement and an eruption of Black social protest. Indeed, a 2017 "Power of the Sister Vote" poll, conducted by the Black Women's Roundtable and *Essence* magazine, found an 11 percent drop between 2016 and 2017 in the support of Black women for the Democratic Party. The poll also reported that the percentage of Black women who feel that neither party supports them had jumped from 13 percent to 21 percent in the same time period.

To anyone who bothered to investigate the conditions in Black communities, these numbers should not be surprising. Looking at Black communities through the specific experiences of Black *women* would have revealed the depths of economic and social crisis unfolding in Black America. Black women had led the way in electoral support for Barack Obama, and with those votes came the expectation that life would improve. Instead of getting better, wages stagnated, poverty increased, and policing was an added burden. These very conditions explain why Black women have led the latest iteration in Black social protest.

We have to stop feeding and fueling the Democratic Party with Black women votes when the Democrats continue to show that they are not concerned with issues affecting Black women. It is my assertion that the focus should not be on the Black folx who choose not to vote because neither party represents our interests. Instead, focus should be directed toward the Democratic Party and the reasons that they have lost our votes, and what, if anything, they are doing to earn our votes back.

SEVENTY-NINE

Grumpy Old White Men

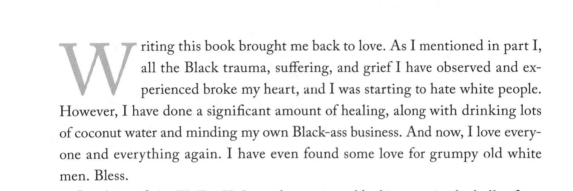

Writing this book brought me back to love. As I mentioned in part I, all the Black trauma, suffering, and grief I have observed and experienced broke my heart, and I was starting to hate white people. However, I have done a significant amount of healing, along with drinking lots of coconut water and minding my own Black-ass business. And now, I love everyone and everything again. I have even found some love for grumpy old white men. Bless.

Speaking of *Are We Free Yet?*, are the grumpy old white men in the halls of our nation's government free yet? No, they are not.

It is my deep Black feminist desire that all white men over the age of sixty-five, in all political parties, offices, and branches of government, retire from running the United States of America, just as they typically do in every other sector of white American life. It is my strong Black feminist wish that grumpy old white men spend the rest of their days golfing somewhere in Florida or the retirement destination of their choice. Let them live out the rest of their days not in my Black-ass business, not in my Black-ass affairs, not speaking on my Black behalf, not making laws for me, and not misrepresenting me at local, state, and national levels. I don't want any grumpy old white men even thinking about me and my Black woman life at all, for any reason, under any circumstances, ever, ever again. Amen.

Can somebody, anybody, throw them an old-school retirement party and release them from their duties?

Where are all the seventy-five-year-old pilots and high school principals and brain surgeons?

Somebody, anybody, please free grumpy old white men from running the country. They have got to be tired too.

Where is the love for grumpy old white men? Why doesn't anyone love them enough to set them free? May they be emancipated from all branches of government. We all should want that for them. And we should want that for us. I submit that if anyone truly loves old white men, then they should stop voting for them so they can stop getting elected and they can go somewhere, sit down, rest . . . however grumpy old white men rest.

EIGHTY

Satan or Lucifer

We lost Congressman John Lewis during the summer of the 2020 up-risings, a grief that was deeply felt among the Black community and anyone who cares about and loves justice.

The last personal memory that I have of him is from when I attended a DNC-sponsored fundraising event for Stacey Abrams for governor in 2018. Pricing for tickets to this event was out of reach for most. I went because someone who had a ticket couldn't go at the last minute but they didn't want their ticket to go to waste, so they gave it to me.

I, along with a few hundred others, watched John Lewis as he danced into the grand ballroom at the Georgia Aquarium to the song "Happy" by Pharrell Williams, next to a tank full of massive white whales that were watching us, knowing that our efforts to save the people with this political party were as effective as the attempts to save the whales (which are still endangered, by the way).

Saving the whales doesn't mean putting them in tanks for formal, elitist dinner party fundraisers. That's enslaving them. Clearly the Democrats didn't understand that. They are playing us. They have been playing us. They are treating us like whales in the aquarium.

So what do you do with a fucked-up two-party system?

You burn it down.

You stop trying to negotiate your humanity with either party.

If there is such a huge difference between the "establishment" Democrats and the Democratic Socialists, then there needs to be an exodus of all Democratic Socialists to form their own party. We need to NOT give our votes to the Democrats this next election cycle just because they are not Republicans.

As a Black feminist, I vehemently believe that supporting any old white man, no matter who he is, will not save us. History shows us what happens with them in charge.

I remember when Donald Trump was just one of about twenty candidates running for the Republican 2016 presidential nomination, and he said that he could shoot someone and still become POTUS. He was right, and even after being president for four years *and* being impeached *twice* and *still* being able to run for president again in 2024, he remains right.

The US would be further along if allies were as antiracist as Trump is racist. I have actually gained a measure of respect for Trump, who has at least been consistent with his bullshit. With his millions of followers, Donald Trump is a mega-brand, and with each outrageous and ridiculous thing he says and does, he strengthens his brand and his base. Those of us who want to fight for freedom from racist systems must keep our focus on the legislation, not on individual politicians and not just on voting blindly for Democrats.

We're not free if all we have are two fucking options and it's voting for either Satan or Lucifer. We *all* know the two-party system needs to change.

JOURNAL PROMPT

What third-party options or political groups are you aware of? Learn about new, different, and radical attempts to establish political power outside of the Republicans and the Democrats. What would it take for you to separate yourself from, or divorce, the Democratic Party?

EIGHTY-ONE

Science, History, Medicine, and Time

Not that long ago, science and history experts gave us three races: the Negroid, the Caucasoid, and the Mongoloid. When I was a little girl, science and medicine said that it was safe to smoke cigarettes . . . on airplanes. Science and medicine also gave us the racist body mass index that is still widely used and accepted today in the nutrition and fitness communities (and the CDC).

Over time, new scientific information has disproved these and many other previously held scientific, historical, and medical "facts."

When I arrived in Montego Bay on July 24, 2020, there had been only twelve COVID-19 deaths in the entire country. Living in Jamaica for that first year of the global pandemic, I watched how this poor, Black country employed a variety of methods to attempt to protect its citizens from catching COVID-19. Two-week quarantines were required for all people flying into the country. A mask mandate was in place countrywide and not negotiable. If you wanted to enter any business, not only did you have to wear a mask (or be denied entry), but many places also took your temperature and required you to sanitize your hands at the door. And for the duration of the time I lived there, a curfew of some sort was always in effect.

Every single day for over a year, everything in the country closed between 6:00 p.m. and 9:00 p.m. in an attempt to slow the spread of the virus. Additionally, throughout 2021, Jamaica had a series of "no-movement lockdowns" that lasted anywhere from one to four days at a time during which businesses were closed and people couldn't go to work or school or even leave our homes (with the exception of foreign travelers with money). These are just some of the biggest ways that the Jamaican government tried to protect the people from COVID-19.

Curfews and lockdowns? American capitalism could never . . . they weren't trying to save lives *that* bad.

By the end of 2021 and the beginning of 2022, along with raising the alarm about the omicron variant, the CDC was busy reminding everyone who the fuck they work for—the Capitalist States of America.

If you ask the millions of Black people why we haven't gotten or aren't getting vaccinated, there are probably millions of different reasons. After all, Black people are not a monolith. But perhaps a great number of the reasons would fall into the categories of scientific racism, historical racism, medical racism, and time.

ACTIVITY

Seek out more information about medical and scientific racism to learn why millions of Black Americans are vaccine hesitant or resistant. Research the following: Henrietta Lacks, The Tuskegee experiment, and visit www.anarchalucybetsey.org.

EIGHTY-TWO

Radical Theory #1

I'm a radical theorist (not to be confused with the flat-earther, variety of conspiracy theorists). The #1 radical theory that I subscribe to is that the US hates Black people. That's it. That's the tweet.

As a queer Black American woman, my worldview has been shaped by that foundational theory. As I have gathered information and done my research on the relationship between the US and us, the descendants of enslaved Africans, all the evidence I have found points in that direction. One of my main takeaways from this theory is be careful what medicine, what narrative, and what benevolence we accept from our enemy. I do not believe the US cares to "save" our lives with a vaccine on Monday just so they can go back to trying to kill us on Tuesday.

Black and marginalized people across the country are dying from COVID-19 at a disproportionately higher rate than rich, white people. But this is no different from every other sector of this Black American life. We are always dying and being targeted and discriminated against at disproportionate rates. This is literally what oppression is and what it does. This is exactly why we are seeking liberation. No matter how dire its effects, the global pandemic is not a unique situation.

The US has effectively already killed us with its racist policies, and it will continue to invent new ways to destroy us. We have to play a different game now, and we must devise tactics that are less conquer and divide and more work together.

How do you get the white liberal Dems to hate and turn against millions of the Black lives they scream matter so much? You introduce a vaccine into the general population and attach to it a narrative of good versus evil, while also knowing that the Black community, with our centuries of being deceived, hoodwinked, bamboozled, and led astray by good old American scientific racism, medical racism, and historical racism, will be hesitant and resistant in taking it. You have now created a situation where the Dems themselves vilify the Black folx whose lives now matter only if they are vaccinated. It's a really simple tactic of divide and conquer. And I have seen its effectiveness as white liberals moved to kick my queer, Black, unvaccinated ass to the curb over this vaccine, as fast as the evangelical Christian church kicks out the gays.

As time goes by, we are learning a lot more about COVID-19 and all its variants. Where there is discrimination happening, let us as activists attack discriminatory policies, not unvaccinated people.

EIGHTY-THREE

Unvaccinated Black Lives
Matter Too

As an antiracism educator and facilitator, racial and social justice advocate and activist, and author, I am one of millions of unvaccinated Black people. I had previously been publicly silent about not getting the vax because I didn't feel that it was necessary to add my unvaccinated voice to the conversation; I have no desire to convince or persuade anyone not to get the vaccine. I don't want to be the champion of the unvaccinated. I feel as strongly today as I have since the vaccine became available that I want everyone to either get the vaccine and boosters, or not get the vaccine and boosters, according to what they feel is best for them, their families, and their communities and what will make them feel safe. Right now, I feel as safe not getting the vaccine as I feel safe being queer and Black and a woman living in the United States of America.

I think that perhaps, had I lived in the States during the first year of the pandemic, I might just have gotten vaccinated without thinking too much about it. But the public dialogue about the vaccine in Jamaica was very different from the shitshow vax discourse that was happening in America.

I don't want to enter into the great debate between the vaxxers and the anti-vaxxers. I don't belong to either of those sides and neither of them speaks for me.

The reason I decided to break my silence about being one of the millions of Black Americans who have not gotten this vaccine is to speak out against the dangerous and racist threat of restricting the rights, access, and movement of un-vaccinated people, which will disproportionately affect black and brown people and other marginalized groups.

There is a difference between saying Black Lives Matter and actually loving Black people.

I just need people who love Black people to stop policing us. Stop policing us in ALL the ways. That includes when it comes to this vaccine.

EIGHTY-FOUR

If I Die of COVID-19 (or Any Other Natural Black Disaster)

Do not blame one single unvaccinated person if I die of COVID-19.

When I die of COVID-19, or any of a number of other natural Black causes, like the effects of poverty, lack of access to healthcare, or police violence (including the public executions that US cops carry out regularly), throw a big fucking party, like the second line of New Orleans. I want much dancing, much eating, much smoking, much fucking. Honor me by honoring you and by honoring us and the time we shared together on this planet that we always knew would come to an end at some point. Keep our memories alive by remembering how we used to be when we were in love, when we were high, when we played in the ocean, when we were envisioning getting free.

A POEM ABOUT FEAR

I am afraid.
But not of catching or dying of
    COVID-19.
I'm afraid of my loved ones leaving me.

I'm not afraid of water in oceans that
    can drown me, that I surf on.
I'm afraid that the people I trust will
    betray me and that I will drown in

their disregard of me and their lack
of loyalty.
I'm not afraid of being in a country
where I don't understand the
language or the culture.
I'm afraid of the country of my birth,
where I understand the language
of lynching and where I see what
they boldly do in the daylight and in
the courtrooms to people who look
like me.
I'm not afraid of being abducted by
Jamaican gangs or drug lords or
Central American crime rings.
I'm afraid of American politicians
and American police bullets
entering my unprotected Black
woman body,
Bullets that go through protected
white walls,
Where protected white females
and their protected white families
sleep,
And those white walls and white
families get a trial
In which no one is found guilty.
I'm afraid of the systems that let us get
sick and offer no medicine.
I'm afraid of the systems that let us
starve while blaming us and
punishing us for being poor.
I'm afraid of the systems that put us
out of housing because jobs don't
pay bills to keep roofs over heads.
I'm not afraid of the unknown,

I'm afraid of what I do know.
Unafraid of what I have not seen,
Afraid of what I have seen.
If I am afraid, it is of my country that
denies Black people justice,
Afraid of my family that abandons me
for being queer,
Afraid of the church that banishes me
to hell made by white Jesus and his
pops.
I don't need protection from those
whom I don't understand, like
speakers of patois in Jamaica or
Spanish in Costa Rica.
I need protection from those whom I
do understand, like those who speak
English in America,
Those who professed love for me only
to stab me in the back and walk
away.
I'm not afraid of Hindu gods or the
Catholic Church.
I'm afraid of the violence of
conservative fundamentalist
Christianity and the lies told to me
in evangelical church walls that
rejected me.
I'm afraid of losing you.
I'm afraid that if I like you too much,
want you too much, care about you
too much, love you,
You will leave me.
I'm afraid of change.
I'm afraid that we are God and we
change and we are the chaos and

the destruction and we are the light
and the creation.
I used to be afraid of everything until I
was lost and discarded so many times
that there was nothing else to lose
and nothing else to be scared of.

**I've lost loved ones to COVID-19,
congestive heart failure,
conservative Christianity, cancer,
car crashes, and cancel culture.**
I've lost a lot. Everyone has.
But I'm just not afraid anymore.

EIGHTY-FIVE

Loving Erica

I was wearing my short red dress with all the parishes of Jamaica on it, surrounded by warm sunset colors and black palm trees. Walking by the pool at my villa, I heard a voice call out to me from the second-floor balcony, "Hey girl! I like your dress!"

After a few kind words exchanged and an introduction, we realized that we had met already in one of our Black expat Facebook groups and had messaged each other about linking up when we were both in Montego Bay. The sisterhood goddesses brought us to live together in the same villa.

Erica Watson was a comedian, a writer, an actress, and a model. She was probably the coolest person I've ever met. You saw her confidence before you saw her fat, light-skinned, barely five-foot Black girl magic body. You heard her voice capturing all your attention before her easy jokes made you full belly laugh.

She was from Chicago. Proudly. She had been hiding out there in her house, trying to wait out the pandemic, but was growing miserable and depressed as the lonely days passed. To save her life, she escaped to Jamaica. Having traveled back and forth to Montego Bay for many years, she knew that the Jamaican sun and air and water and food would be good for her health and her mental state. So she decided to come to the island to wait out COVID-19.

And with a fine twenty-five-year-old Jamaican boyfriend by her side, here she was as my neighbor at Black Melrose Place.

Upon meeting and kiki-ing like new Black girlfriends do, we decided to go to Dead End Beach the next night. Her boyfriend drove us to the Hip Strip, where he parked and we walked up to an outdoor bar and grill. We placed our orders and took our very first round of pictures.

Erica was always camera-ready. And the camera was always Erica-ready. Her short hair was a fading, shock pink color. She wore a tie-dye tank top, jeans, and black sneakers. I wore my long, sleeveless purple muumuu. With a strawberry daiquiri in her hand and a woven backpack on my shoulders, we posed as her boyfriend snapped several shots of us together.

At Black Melrose Place, Erica mostly kept the front door to her studio apartment open to welcome in the Caribbean breeze. In the mornings, I could hear her and her boyfriend talking and laughing as he prepared to leave for work at the airport, only after making her a breakfast of fresh fruit. I would greet her as I returned from my two-mile walk each morning in our neighborhood. She spent most of the day on the phone or computer with her clients, her agents, her parents, her brother, her friends. She was always in writing and planning mode . . . writing a play that she was submitting to a contest, planning her podcast and YouTube show. We would invite each other to meet up in the pool midafternoons or early evenings, where we would spend time just wading and listening to West African or reggae music, while I smoked spliffs. She told me she couldn't get high as she had tried and been unsuccessful in the past. This presented us with a fun challenge and we made a few attempts to get her high, which I think happened only once.

We became fast friends. She was so easy to love.

EIGHTY-SIX

One Love

Two days before my six-month visitor visa in Jamaica expired and I had to return to the States, my friend Cole took me and two of my friends to Benta River Falls. I spent that afternoon high, swimming in the cool Jamaican river waters with these two beautiful queer Black women and this one beautiful cis-het Black man whom I have known all my life (because Cole reminded me of every Black man that I had ever met), and I felt like I was in love with all three of them at the same time. We were in the water, in the sun, in our bodies. Love was in the air. Love was on the tips of our ganja-stained lips and tongues. Love was in the laughter of the children jumping into the river from ropes tied to elder trees on the riverbank. Love was when we held hands to help each other move from one slippery river stone to the next. We were getting through the river in community. We helped each other. We delighted in the river and in our delightful Black selves. Our slick skin rubbed together over and over again. I felt like I belonged to all of them and to each of them. I felt like we belonged to one another as much as we belonged to ourselves. I felt no jealousy here, no competition, no desire for owning. It felt like the closest thing to perfect love casting out fear that I had ever experienced. And those were the waves and the sensations that I rode in my head and in my heart and in my body all day long.

Later that night when we returned to Black Melrose Place, someone suggested that we do ecstasy. And so within a few hours, my friends and I were upstairs on the balcony at Black Melrose Place overlooking the pool. The sun had just set, nightfall was fresh, and for the first time since COVID-19, there was a party happening down around the pool; the owner had invited all the guests who were staying at the villa to a cookout.

My friends and I sat up there on that balcony around the table with candles lit, incense burning, and music playing. I remember looking down at everyone gathered by the pool, celebrating for absolutely no other reason than that it was another day in paradise. I could see my dear friend Erica and her boyfriend sitting around one of the tables. I could see the guests who were staying downstairs who were rumored to be drug dealers and who kept a steady flow of sex workers with them. I could see my Jamaican friends walking around, serving up the escovitch fish to the guests, freshly grilled. There were rum bottles and the particular ring of heavy patois being spoken. Everyone looked lit up like Christmas trees. Everything was ablaze. My skin started to burn and it was so delicious and tantalizing that I realized and declared to my friends, to everyone in Jamaica, and most importantly to myself, for the first time, that I am the sun.

In those moments, I affirmed myself and my decision to move to Jamaica. There was no place I'd rather be. And I am convinced that there was no other place that Erica would have chosen to be in that moment on that day either.

Five weeks later, she would die of complications from COVID-19.

A POEM ABOUT LAST NIGHT

Last night felt holy and sacred, and not
    to write about it would be a sin.
A small, covered, outdoor space,
A small gathering of humans
Eating food cooked by warm hands
    and soft hearts.
Pumpkin soup, fritters, cornbread
    muffins.
Varying types of rum in varying types
    of beverages.
Ting, ginger beer, cubes of ice.

Songs from an iPhone on the speaker,
    switching abruptly before the song
    was over, while we were still
    singing.
Dancing in our chairs and stools.
The leaves on the native trees around
    us alerting us to the rain. It felt like
    we were in the trees, not just among
    them.
Ganja smoke all around, mine and
    theirs. Spliffs offered and passed.

Herb gratefully inhaled. Pleasure gracefully exhaled.

It was the peaceful energy for me.

Varying shades of skin, hair, and accents.

Discussions of music making or maybe lovemaking. You gotta watch this. Listen to this. Can you play this song? And if the crowd stops moving, just play Bruno Mars.

Legs touching.

Eyes scanning.

Taking it all in.

I was drunk in love and contentment.

Laughter and posturing.

Patois and the king's English.

Locs standing straight up, falling down on shoulders, and wrapped around and up.

Fresh braids too tight.

Ponytails and shaved heads.

An old, not pregnant cat.

It felt like friendship and smelled like the sunset.

Room temperature tap water in my wineglass.

My feet swollen from the rum.

He offered to carry me on his back.

And the rest only my heart knows.

EIGHTY-SEVEN

Losing Erica

It was just a few short weeks before she died that I hugged her goodbye on my way to the airport, and she promised me that she would be there to greet me when I returned. As she saw me off, in her classic joking way she gave me permission to hug her new husband goodbye . . . because he was young and fine as hell and she did not play when it came to her man!

Erica and I texted the whole time I was in the States; she texted me when she got sick, and right up until the day she died. I returned to our Jamaican home a week later and my body and heart hadn't fully grasped what my mind knew because everywhere I turned, I saw and felt her right where she had been since she walked into my villa back in October. We had been together pretty much every day since. We were always talking and laughing and plotting and planning. We were reveling and beaming and literally GLOWING in the fact that we had got ourselves free and she had found love. Randomly throughout the day we would call-and-respond to each other, "Guurrl, we live in fucking Jamaica!" We would tsk and hmph and giggle like schoolgirls. We would wade in the pool, sometimes gossiping about the other guests at the villa.

We shared about our former relationships and heartbreak, and she was the kind of friend that became so protective of me that she wanted to kick Dawn's ass (let's just say she helped me find some of my ancestral Chicago anger, lol). On a daily basis, we were bearing witness to each other's physical and emotional healing. She was the friend who was promoting me even when I never asked her to, and sometimes I didn't even know when she was doing it. I remember her telling me one day out of the blue to be sure I posted a bunch of IG stories for a four-day period because she had pitched me to Facebook for a project.

She had me as a guest on her late-night YouTube show the night before I flew back to the States. And on that show, she talked a little bit about the love she and I shared as new friends who felt more like old sisters. Many nights (after she spent the day writing and working hard for her clients), she would hit me up to go for a drive with her and her then boyfriend. We would end up in Granville or in the hour-long line at the KFC drive-thru (that might not even have chicken by the time we got up to the window), but mostly we would go to Dead End Beach, which was one of our favorite spots.

She was the kind of friend I could call to go and retrieve my sex toys that I had forgotten in the nightstand drawer in my room before the housekeeper found them and threw them away. She gave me tremendous insight into the Jamaican dating scene (as she had come back and forth to JA for many years) while also telling me that I was emasculating to men, presenting me with the receipts—all the dudes who had tried it with me and got shut down swiftly. She was beautiful and bold and unapologetic and confident in a way that I have never been but always wanted to be. She would *say the thing* that everyone was thinking but no one else would dare say. And we loved her for that. She had an effortless way of making you laugh but not just in her professional comedian kind of way, more often in that "Girl, that is so true" or in the "I can't believe Erica just said that" way. I felt comfortable and safe with her, and I suspect the friends she had for years would say the same.

We truly saw each other and enjoyed one another's company, and we talked at length about what it meant for us to be living our best lives right now, here in JA, during the time of COVID-19. We talked about COVID-19 a lot. She took it very seriously and she was very careful, we all were, especially because we were in each other's pod and understood her health risks.

Remembering some of those conversations we had about COVID-19 is especially painful for me right now because it turns out that she was very right, and I was very wrong. She told me often how grateful she was to be here even though she missed her family and friends in Chicago. On Christmas Day, we ate a Sri Lankan meal together that our dear friend, Sonali, made for us with love. She talked about writing a script about our experiences healing and growing and loving in Jamaica. We both shared our hopes and dreams of bringing other Black American women to Jamaica to experience this particular kind of Jamaican joy. She was the only one on the planet who knew ALL the details of my queer, poly, pansexual adventures and situation-ships around the island, and some of those stories have gone with her to her grave. Because if she can't tell them in her classic Erica way, I don't even want them told.

It feels good to talk about my friend as the tears start to come again. Her words, her face, and her voice are still on my phone. These are only a few of the many special moments that we shared. I'm sure I will share more at some point. But for now, this is how I'm remembering my friend, the way we were on so many MoBay days and nights.

Erica was truly passionate about being in Jamaica, and she was very much in love and very much loved and adored by her husband. I will never forget the moment when, as I sat next to her in my apartment just a few minutes before leaving for the airport, she whispered in my ear that they had gotten married.

I had watched him love her every single day, all the way to the end. She talked about keeping their marriage a secret for a while because people can be cruel and wouldn't want to believe that a big girl like her could get a hot Jamaican man like him. I respected that and I will now cherish the pictures she sent me of them getting married three days earlier at a local church. When she did share the news of her marriage later on Facebook, she referenced a friend who burst into tears of joy upon hearing the news . . . that friend was me. I hear her voice in my head right now telling me (all of us really) to live my best life and enjoy myself because life is short. I will honor Erica's memory and legacy for as many days as I have left. I will always love you, Erica, and may you rest well knowing you gave all of us who knew you and even so many who didn't know you full love, full laughter, and full joy.

ARTIFACT
Last Text Messages from Erica

February 27, 2021, 12:48 p.m.

FULL PRAYER NEEDED NOW TO 90% OXYGEN OR I BE BUT
IM FULL COMA TONIGHT. PLEASE PRAY NOW 90% by next 2
jours. I qm at 75% now. I can beay this!!!!!!!!!!

12:49 p.m.

I do not want to be in a coma with a breathing tube. Please help
me!!!! Please help me!!!! Um begging

Erica's oxygen did not get up to 90 percent.
She died later that night, as soon as they put her on a ventilator, against her will.

ACTIVITY

Learn more about Erica's work, life, and legacy of laughter and love by going to Google and
YouTube and searching "Erica Faye Watson."

A POEM ABOUT JAMAICA

When we say "live our best life," let us
   take this as a war cry.
Our ancestors are shouting this.
We are shouting this back to
   ourselves, in our own voices, from
   the other side.
As in live your best life right now.
There is no need to choose between
   caring about your community and
   living your best life.
You can do both.
Find your community.

Find your people.
Erica found hers here with us.
I returned to Jamaica at the beginning
   of March . . .
Days after Erica died.
Days after my second divorce was
   finalized.
I was a mess. Again.
In these past three months I have
   grown older and wiser on the inside,
   while growing younger and stronger
   on the outside.

I prioritized building community.
I manifested more epic shit.
I got back in therapy.
Every single person who crossed my
    path has been a gift or a lesson.

The ganja and Caribbean waters
    sustained me and revived my
    spirit through MoBay days and
    nights.
Thank you for all of it, Jamaica.

EIGHTY-EIGHT

Alive

I have walked that long road to freedom. I have tried not to falter; I have made missteps along the way. But I have discovered the secret that after climbing a great hill, one only finds that there are many more hills to climb. I have taken a moment here to rest, to steal a view of the glorious vista that surrounds me, to look back on the distance I have come. But I can rest only for a moment, for with freedom come responsibilities, and I dare not linger, for my long walk is not ended.

—NELSON MANDELA

A friend told me that I am her most alive friend, and I love that so much because it reminds me that all I truly want and aim to be is alive.

I chose to leave the US to do that. I chose to go on hiatus from my antiracism work immediately after George Floyd was killed, because that cop's knee on his neck and those cop bullets that entered Breonna Taylor's body made me realize something, that I will not let *fighting* white supremacy kill me. The reality is that white supremacy might just kill us anyway as it has killed millions of Black and Indigenous folx since racist European feet got lost and landed here/there/everywhere around the globe. To the best of our ability, we need to live intentionally, and as powerfully, courageously, unapologetically, and revolutionarily as we can, with every second of this blessed Black life that we have been given.

We find our way. Somehow, in our fight for liberation, and in our fight to live, we figure out how to navigate and get along with the multitude of oppressive barriers that stand between us and freedom. Along the way, we discover that people will disappoint us, judge us, and stop loving us. And we discover that though we may blame others for abandoning us, it is actually we who abandon ourselves more than anyone else.

Angela Davis said, "Freedom is a constant struggle."

I no longer believe that we get to complete freedom on this side of breath and skin and bones. Not in these bodies. Not with these borders. Not with these hierarchies. Not in all the ways that we hope and dream of.

Are we free yet? Some days my answer is yes. Other days it's no. Some days I just don't know.

We all must answer this question of freedom for ourselves. Constantly. And we must ask freedom questions. Constantly. Until we know for sure.

EIGHTY-NINE

Being a Liberation Activist

L iberation is ultimately a celebration of our deepest humanity, and our fight for it must include a deeper examination of how we relate to oppressive systems while centering our joy, peace, and pleasure.

All of us interact with liberation and oppression at all times every day, whether we are conscious of it or not. Freedom is a practice. It is a delicate and complex dance routine and, like your body, must be used and exercised to reach its full potential. Freedom is movement . . . a living, breathing thing that must be protected and preserved, embodied and believed.

Freedom costs something. But so does oppression. Owning the rights to ourselves and our stories costs quite a lot. We set the value for our freedom by deciding what it costs us, and we reinforce that value in the ways in which we assert our freedom. The systems that work together to uphold racial, gender, and social hierarchies are the ones that we live and move and breathe with every day.

But oppression does not have to be what defines us.

White supremacy is a practice. Many have also made it a religion that they worship and sacrifice to all day, every day. It requires active participation and affirmation. White supremacy culture exists only because of the repetitive affirming of it.

The same is true of liberation.

In our daily lives we can observe the ways in which our relationships with our spouses and partners, our country and ourselves, are either surrendering to oppression or striving toward liberation.

By identifying what freedom and oppression feel like, we are able to begin to understand which ways of being are best suited for our joy and our humanity. We identify our feelings of freedom through our ability to access joy. If we can't identify our feelings of being stuck, enslaved, or oppressed, we won't be able to understand how we are participating in our own oppression.

In all our movement, our music, art, dancing, love, and radical ways, we are reclaiming life. We are reclaiming our humanity.

NINETY

Write Your Own
Declaration of Liberation

For some of us, it isn't possible to find freedom by knocking on doors in the hallways of oppression. For some of us, finding freedom means lighting a match, setting that bitch on fire, and walking out of the burning building altogether (cue our favorite scene of Angela Bassett lighting her cheating husband's car on fire and walking away in the classic Black movie *Waiting to Exhale*). There must come a point where we stop asking if we can pull up a chair to their oppressive tables. We must stop asking those who sit in power if we can please have our freedom back.

It is a lie that we must seek the benevolence of our oppressors in hopes of being granted our freedom.

We must take our freedom for ourselves.

We must not agree that they hold the power by asking them to stop oppressing us.

We must demand our freedom.

We must assume our freedom.

We must empower ourselves to get ourselves fucking free.

No person can give another person freedom unless the unfree person agrees that their freedom belongs to the person whom they are asking their freedom from.

Who is it that you must ask for your freedom?

Who holds the keys to unlock the chains to your personal jail cell and mental captivity?

Who do you need to get permission from to walk away from a relationship with an abuser?

When will you be free?

Is it when the president of the United States says you are free?

Is it when your boss at work says you are free?

Is it when your husband says you are free?

If you don't like being enslaved, to whom must you appeal to get your freedom back?

What is their name?

Where do they live and work?

When did you give them your power?

And most importantly, how will you take it back?

JOURNAL PROMPT

Answer the previous questions in the declaration of liberation that you must write for and deliver to yourself. Write your freedom papers, friend.

NINETY-ONE

White People for Black Lives: Educate Yourself

> Whites, it must frankly be said, are not putting in a similar mass effort to reeducate themselves out of their racial ignorance. It is an aspect of their sense of superiority that the white people of America believe they have so little to learn.
>
> —MARTIN LUTHER KING JR.

As white people who love Black people and are committed to fighting for our lives, bring your heart into the work of antiracism, but also bring your head by arming yourself with knowledge. Prioritize educating yourself. This is where you move from spectator to student. Step back and realize that the oppression and racism you are passionate about ending are multifaceted and nuanced issues. Come into the work with a determination not to be willfully ignorant about the cause you care about. Enter into the space with humility. While you have much to contribute to the cause, you first have much to learn. Your entry point into the work is important, but cultivating respect for the cause and for those who have paved the way and have already been engaged in the work is critical. Any social justice progress that has been made up to this point is due to the labor, time, and literal sweat, blood, and tears of so many people who have come before you. Honor the groundwork that has been laid by studying to find out who is most affected, what the struggle has looked like, and how far it has come. Familiarize yourself with the opposition so you can speak to a variety of perspectives from an informed and well-rounded place. Educating yourself will allow you to appreciate the dynamics of an issue in order to gain a better understanding of the scope of the work and where you will fit into it.

Educating yourself will take initiative on your part. Don't expect anyone to educate you as this is your responsibility and a sign that you take this seriously. This step is all about listening and learning.

There are many injustice-impacted folx who are doing the work of providing education for social justice advocates. These justice mentors and guides are gifts to humanity. They are here to help you on your education path; however, those who have been called to serve the collective in this way must be acknowledged, appreciated, and paid for their work. In order to break the cycle of exploitation and stolen labor, you must prioritize paying your educators for their time, emotional labor, and wisdom. Compensation must be a foundational pillar of your social justice work, and that doesn't include well-meaning gestures like inviting someone to lunch. It means exchanging currency for resources.

Please note that when directly impacted folx share their stories, it can be triggering for them and you. Keep in the forefront of your mind that people have experienced trauma and violence in a variety of ways, and retelling those experiences is not something that everyone wants or needs to do. Most importantly, it should not be necessary for someone to expose their trauma to you for you to care about an issue.

You don't have to personally identify with the affected group for which you are advocating. The goal here is not to become an expert but to become an advocate. The experts are those who have been most affected by injustice. Be intentional in seeking out the guidance, direction, leadership, and wisdom of BIPOC who live on the margins and at the intersections of discrimination and oppression and whose lived experience makes them experts. When you enter into a fight for justice, you are arriving as a guest first.

NINETY-TWO

White People, Take Action

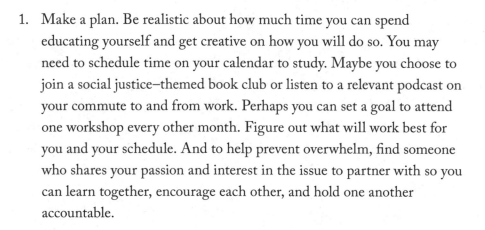

1. Make a plan. Be realistic about how much time you can spend educating yourself and get creative on how you will do so. You may need to schedule time on your calendar to study. Maybe you choose to join a social justice–themed book club or listen to a relevant podcast on your commute to and from work. Perhaps you can set a goal to attend one workshop every other month. Figure out what will work best for you and your schedule. And to help prevent overwhelm, find someone who shares your passion and interest in the issue to partner with so you can learn together, encourage each other, and hold one another accountable.

2. Seek out reputable sources to get your information. Consider hiring someone, an antiracism coach or consultant, to help with this. Join a local or virtual advocacy group or organization.

3. Learn about the legislation and current laws and policies that are in place (or not in place) affecting your chosen social justice issue. Find out which elected officials support and oppose social justice reforms, whether it's a local or national issue or both. Voting and holding elected

officials accountable for addressing your concerns as one of their constituents can be very effective in bringing about change.

4. Invest in mutual aid and advocate for income redistribution, land tax, and reparation models that put money directly into the hands of Black people and families.

NINETY-THREE

I Am Not Your Resource

I am not your resource.

I am a person. People can be teachers, educators, facilitators, healers, coaches, and so forth.

Resources come in many forms such as books, documentaries, and multimedia content.

Resources are available and accessible 24/7. People are not.

Resources do not have feelings. People do.

Resources can't be triggered or traumatized. People can be.

Some great places to get connected to your favorite educators and resources are classes, workshops, conferences, conventions, Patreon, and social media platforms and communities. (Please be sure you are paying your educators and teachers, especially if they are BIPOC.)

People PROVIDE resources. But we are not resources ourselves.

Normalize seeing and celebrating us in our full humanity.

NINETY-FOUR

The Liberation of Mutual Aid

L earn about and invest significantly in mutual aid. Instead of giving money to politicians, candidates, and political parties, give money directly to BIPOC and LGBTQIA+ individuals or orgs that you follow and learn from and who are helping to save lives.

In April 2019, I got two driving violations in Milton, Georgia, for driving with expired tags and not having car insurance.

Technically, I lived in unincorporated Fulton County, right on the border of Alpharetta and Milton. The Milton police were sitting at the intersection, running people's tags and pulling them over as they waited at the stop light near the apartment complex where I lived. They gave me two tickets, and then after explaining to me that they really should impound my car and take me to jail, they allowed me to park my car in my garage (since we were right next to my apartment), but they took my license plate so I couldn't drive my car until I had taken care of the tickets.

This put me, as a poor person, in a situation where I was working full-time to barely pay my bills but now I no longer had a vehicle to get myself to and from work. Fortunately, a dear Black woman friend of mine let me borrow her extra car so I didn't have to pay to rent a car or take public transportation. That was a blessing, and another one of the millions of ways Black women have saved me.

(Quick question: How many poor Black people do you think can just borrow a friend's extra car at no cost to get to and from work for a few weeks?)

In this particular situation, we were struggling financially because we were supporting two households. I lived in Fulton County and worked as a general manager at a privately owned (chain) gym, while Dawn lived in San Antonio where she was finishing her software engineer boot camp. I used to "ride dirty" from time to time because I didn't always have the money to pay everything on time; sometimes I had to rob Peter to pay Paul when it came to monthly bills. This was during one of the times that auto insurance was not the lucky winner when I worked out which bills would get paid that month—a not-so-fun game that poor Americans play.

When I went to court, I asked to make payment arrangements to cover my fines. I was told that being on a payment arrangement would mean that I would be placed on probation. This involved an additional cost: each month I would be forced to meet with a probation officer and pay a probation fee until I paid off the $750 cost of the tickets. And of course, I also still had to pay to get my tags and auto insurance renewed.

This amount of money (and being placed on probation for being poor) was completely overwhelming for me. I sat in my car in the parking lot of the office of the City of Milton and sobbed for about an hour. I just didn't have the $750 to take care of the fine immediately. And I didn't want to be on probation, couldn't be on probation, because we were moving back to Texas in a few weeks, where Dawn would be starting a new tech job.

So I considered sitting in jail to pay off my fines.

I posted about this on my Facebook page and a rich white ally, who didn't want to see me as a queer Black woman sitting in a cage for any reason, but especially not because I couldn't afford to pay my tickets, messaged me on Facebook privately. She asked if she could lend me the full $750 to pay off my fines so that I wouldn't have to consider sitting in jail. I gratefully accepted her offer and she sent me the money, with only two requests of me: to keep her name anonymous, and to pay the $750 back, not to her directly but to justice organizations that I loved.

And that's exactly what I did.

That practice actually started me on my own giving journey. As a result of receiving that financial blessing-miracle, I did pay that initial $750 that she gave me back to groups that I cared about: the Equal Justice Initiative and the National Bail Out, a Black-women-led organization that helps bail out of jail Black mothers and caregivers who can't afford to post bail and provides them support after they've been locked up. But even when I paid off that amount, I kept on giving. I kept finding organizations that I trusted to give money to.

With the help of the supporters of the *Speaking of Racism* podcast, that Mother's Day, we raised money for the National Bail Out. We were able to send them a few thousand dollars, which was double what I had been able to help give the previous year. But then I started giving money here and there to individuals, prioritizing queer Black people. When I heard that a Black trans formerly incarcerated person needed funds, someone who had been bullied, harassed, and threatened by the followers of a very public and popular mixed-race male in the social justice space who had been lying about and causing harm to Black women for years, I gave. And when a family member of mine experiencing hate from other family members due to their sexuality needed money, I gave.

And when a Black trans woman needed cash, I gave.

And I kept finding Black folx to give money to, and it became one of my spiritual practices.

Growing up in the church, I was raised to tithe to the church. Now, since I no longer go to church (or subscribe to any organized, white supremacist, patriarchal religion), I pay my tithes directly to Black people, especially Black trans people. Because trans people are holy and divine.

ACTIVITY

If you are a someone with financial privilege, make a list of 1-5 Black people you can give money to on a monthly basis for no reason and with no expectation to receive anything in return.

NINETY-FIVE

Poor People Shit

This spiritual practice of giving money to Black women allowed me to honor my younger self: the me I was as a single mom with three kids living in Houston.

In 2010, I was running one of the largest fitness programs in the Houston region for LA Fitness, and then I took a significant pay cut when I started working for Life Time Fitness. I was barely making enough money to take care of all four of us on an annual salary of around $40,000. We struggled financially, so much so that I had a lot of creative ways to make ends meet. One of those creations was a system I developed of "floating" checks at Walmart to get us through between paychecks.

With approximately thirty dollars in my checking account, I would buy exactly thirty dollars' worth of groceries, and then at the register, I would write a check for sixty dollars to get thirty dollars cash back so I could put gas in my car until payday. And since floating checks was a thing back then, I learned that I needed only half the amount of the funds requested in order to have the bank not reject the check. This would generate a thirty-dollar non-sufficient funds fee from the bank, which would make my account overdrawn (and God forbid it was time for some automatic bill to go through—then I might be paying multiple NSF fees) for borrowing money from myself. This was how I got by, this was how I took care of myself and my three kids.

When my kids were in junior high and high school in Keller, Texas, I often relied on the local churches and organizations which gave us free boxed holiday meals and allowed me to go through their makeshift Christmas shop to get gifts for my kids that I otherwise just couldn't afford. And this was when I was teaching group fitness classes six to seven days a week to rich white people, whose children my own kids went to school with every day. No one knew that's what I was going through. There is so much shame wrapped up in being Black and poor and single.

It wasn't until years later when Chelsea had graduated from Baylor University and was working for the Texas Hunger Initiative in Waco that she made me aware that our little family was what they call food insecure.

This is why I give money to Black people. Because I remember what just thirty or fifty dollars would have meant to me, to us, if I had received it unexpectedly or out of the blue. It would have made the difference between having to float another check until payday and not having my account go negative again. It would have made the difference of still having that thirty-dollar NSF fee in my pocket to go toward taking care of us, rather than to the banking institution that rapes all of us with their fees.

And receiving an extra thirty to fifty dollars would have also made a difference to my own mother, who was a teacher for almost twenty years for the Dallas Independent School District. Also working full-time, my own mother was another Black college graduate who wasn't making enough of a salary to pay all the bills all the time. I declare that if you have never felt THAT level of financial despair, if you have never spent years living below the poverty line as I have, if you have never been food or housing insecure like I was, then you may not be able to understand or relate to why I have gone through everything I have gone through to get free, and to try all these wild and radical strategies to get myself free so I can show others that freedom is possible.

I am getting myself free so that when my kids have kids of their own, they don't have to barely live, being barely able to make ends meet, like I did. If you don't know what it's like to live paycheck to paycheck as a single parent, then perhaps you don't know how not free that feels. And you can't know, like poor Black folx know, that once you feel that enslaved and helpless, you will do almost anything not to feel that way ever again.

If you have been blessed financially, or if someone else has been a financial blessing to you, I ask that you consider giving directly to individuals who need money. I invite you to make mutual aid one of your spiritual practices.

NINETY-SIX

Never Stop Listening to and Learning from Black Women

Find Black women leaders and activists to follow, listen to, and learn from, and to support financially as you are able. Black women have been and are still leading the way forward when it comes to organizing social justice movements and so much more. But all too often, our voices and contributions have been overlooked, flat-out ignored, co-opted by dominant culture, and erased. Black queer and trans womxn and femmes are historically some of the most underpaid, devalued, and at-risk folx in our society. One of the greatest opportunities for getting free that we have is to be intentional in seeking out Black queer and trans folx to lead the way as we work to dismantle oppressive structures and systems and envision and create equitable ones to replace them.

ARTIFACT
Excerpts from the Combahee River Collective Statement

The most general statement of our politics at the present time would be that we are actively committed to struggling against racial, sexual, heterosexual, and class oppression, and see as our particular task the development of integrated analysis and practice based upon the fact that the major systems of oppression are interlocking . . .

. . . As Angela Davis points out in "Reflections on the Black Woman's Role in the Community of Slaves," Black women have always embodied, if only in their physical manifestation, an adversary stance to white male rule and have actively resisted its inroads upon them and their communities in both dramatic and subtle ways. There have always been Black women activists—some known, like Sojourner Truth, Harriet Tubman, Frances E. W. Harper, Ida B. Wells Barnett, and Mary Church Terrell, and thousands upon thousands unknown—who have had a shared awareness of how their sexual identity combined with their racial identity to make their whole life situation and the focus of their political struggles unique . . .

. . . Many of us were active in those movements (Civil Rights, Black nationalism, the Black Panthers), and all of our lives were greatly affected and changed by their ideologies, their goals, and the tactics used to achieve their goals. It was our experience and disillusionment within these liberation movements, as well as experience on the periphery of the white male left, that led to the need to develop a politics that was antiracist, unlike those of white women, and antisexist, unlike those of Black and white men.

There is also undeniably a personal genesis for Black feminism, that is, the political realization that comes from the seemingly personal experiences of individual Black women's lives . . .

Above all else, our politics initially sprang from the shared belief that Black women are inherently valuable, that our liberation is a necessity not as an adjunct to somebody else's but because of our need as human persons for autonomy . . . We realize that the only people who care enough about us to work consistently for our liberation are us . . .

This focusing upon our own oppression is embodied in the concept of identity politics. We believe that the most profound and potentially most radical politics come directly out of our own identity, as opposed to working to end somebody else's oppression . . .

We believe that sexual politics under patriarchy is as pervasive in Black women's lives as are the politics of class and race . . .

. . . We struggle together with Black men against racism, while we also struggle with Black men about sexism.

We realize that the liberation of all oppressed peoples necessitates the destruction of the political-economic systems of capitalism and imperialism as well as patriarchy. We are socialists because we believe that work must be organized for the collective benefit of those who do the work and create the products, and not for the profit of the bosses . . .

A political contribution which we feel we have already made is the expansion of the feminist principle that the personal is political . . .

The psychological toll of being a Black woman and the difficulties this presents in reaching political consciousness and doing political work can never be underestimated . . .

. . . If Black women were free, it would mean that everyone else would have to be free since our freedom would necessitate the destruction of all the systems of oppression.

. . . Here is the way male and female roles were defined in a Black nationalist pamphlet from the early 1970s:

We understand that it is and has been traditional that the man is the head of the house. He is the leader of the house/nation because his knowledge of the world is broader, his awareness is greater, his understanding is fuller and his application of this information is wiser . . . After all, it is only reasonable that the man be the head of the house because he is able to defend and protect the development of his home . . . Women cannot do the same things as men—they are made by nature to function differently. Equality of men and women is something that cannot happen even in the abstract world. Men are not equal to other men, i.e., ability, experience or even understanding. The value of men and women can be seen as in the value of gold and silver—they are not equal but both have great value. We must realize that men and women are a complement to each other because there is no house/family without a man and his wife. Both are essential to the development of any life.

. . . Many Black women have a good understanding of both sexism and racism, but, because of the everyday constrictions of their lives, cannot risk struggling against them both.

The reaction of Black men to feminism has been notoriously negative. They are, of course, even more threatened than Black women by the possibility that Black feminists might organize around our own needs. They realize that they might not only lose valuable and hardworking allies in their struggles but that they might also be forced to change their habitually sexist ways of interacting with and oppressing Black women.

NINETY-SEVEN

Closure

February 26, 2021, 1:17 p.m.

Dawn, I wouldn't change anything about the seven and a half years we spent together.

I would change everything about what happened to us AFTER Seattle.

We died on that mat. I said goodbye to you there. The you I knew and loved for so long.

I accept that we are done, I wasn't sure if I had any last words for you after all I've said before. But I do, these are those final words. We were something, we were real and you disrespected love. Not marriage. But love. Treat Black women better this time.

T hat was the text message I sent to Dawn after receiving her text message telling me that our divorce had been finalized. She responded by apologizing for the way things had ended and for hurting me. I knew I would not be able to absorb what she was saying for a while. I called up a friend and told them about my divorce being final and said that I wanted to do some kind of grief ceremony, in the woods, about an hour north of Atlanta, back in East Cobb, at the Gold Branch Trail, to be exact. That was the trail in the neighborhood where we used to live, the neighborhood where she loved me and kept me warm, when two of my three kids still lived with us and attended high school. It was the trail near what I used to call our "tree house dream house." It was where we were living when we found out that Chaz had died. It was where all three of our kids had a big house party when Dawn and I were in Anguilla for a wedding. That house was where I smoked weed and got high for the first time. It was where I flew my three oldest nephews in from Dallas to be with us so we could have a big family Christmas gathering and re-create a picture of the six cousins that was originally taken seventeen years earlier. It was the house where we lived when I accidentally watched the videos of Philando Castile and Alton Sterling being killed by police. It was where my happy trees turned our backyard into a jungle and where deer came to visit us.

It was the house where we lived when I had a very difficult breakup with my white best friend of ten years because when I told her I was concerned that despite the fact that there were Black bus drivers and Black cafeteria workers and Black janitors at my son's high school (Walton High School in East Cobb), there were no Black teachers or Black administrators, she responded that solving the problem couldn't mean discriminating against the white teachers because it would be unfair for them to lose their jobs and retirement just so the district could hire Black teachers. It was the house where I lived when I helped open a boutique cycle studio around the corner, teaching classes for two years and creating a community among the riders. It was the house where our sweet puppy, Jax, joined our family for our first Christmas in Georgia.

It was 4,300 square feet, three stories, four bedrooms, and four bathrooms of love.

So I needed to return to the place where our love had lived so that I could say goodbye.

A year and a half after she left me, Dawn emailed me some letters she had written to me that first week we were separated but never sent. They were beautiful in a way that made me feel seen by her, which was all I had ever wanted. Isn't that all we really want from those we love? There has been closure for us. There may be more to this story at some point. Or there may not be. I'm at peace either way, and I hope she is at peace too.

What kind of closure do you want or need? Do you think you could benefit your healing and liberation journey by writing an apology or a closure letter? To an ex-spouse, a former friend, or a family member? To yourself? If so, write it now. If you need to take your time with this, set a goal to finish it by a date over the next thirty days and hold yourself accountable for completing this forgiveness exercise.

NINETY-EIGHT

Saying Goodbye

Living in America, there came a point when I realized that the good days no longer outweighed the bad days. By the time I finally walked away, I was so bruised and broken that there was little love left. Almost none to speak of. That was when I knew it was time for me to say goodbye.

Beloveds, if your spirit is telling you, has been telling you, to leave that abusive relationship, then leave you must. You owe yourself a chance at freedom. You deserve the right to find peace and have abundant joy. Don't suffocate yourself there. Leave before you start to hate. There is so much more space for forgiveness and healing. So leave before the hate sets in and destroys you, because hate is also a form of oppression.

How do you know when it's time to say goodbye? I think that it is when we start to count all the pieces of our broken heart, when we realize the truth about where we are and what this relationship has become. When we accept the truth about what has changed, or rather, what has stayed the same. When we take a step back, are able to acknowledge our delusion, and separate fact from fiction, what we want and wish for versus what is.

If you have found yourself at the intersection of staying or leaving, recognize that it is only you who brought you here to this point of decision, and there are no easy ones. This is why our first step is to grieve. Because there is much to grieve, likely more than we can even comprehend. We must grieve what we thought it was, and all that has taken place. Grieve all the shades of Black trauma. Grieve the abandonment and the betrayal. Grieve the Black lives lost. Grieve the love denied, the love withheld. And then decide to save yourself and become your own fucking liberator.

My ancestors are crying out in my soul, pleading with me to find my peace in another country. What is being asked of me is to trust, have faith, say goodbye, and take the jump.

My path, like the paths of millions of other Black folx who are sick and tired of being sick and tired, has led me to other lands in search of a peace and freedom that does not exist for me in my homeland.

What is being asked of you?

NINETY-NINE

Dear America

I love America more than any other country in the world, and, exactly for
this reason, I insist on the right to criticize her perpetually.

—JAMES BALDWIN

Dear America,

I have written this book about why I must divorce you, full of reasons
and artifacts and lists that I've compiled after forty-two years of living
with you. And though it may seem that I was the one to leave you, after reviewing
all my evidence and data, I've come to the conclusion that it was you who abandoned me first.

When you set out to divorce England, you tried to start over, to start something
new and do it better, but you failed before you even began. You built, as we used
to sing in Sunday school, your house not upon the rock but upon the sand. Your
very first promise was also your very first lie: to recognize that we are all endowed
with the unalienable rights of life, liberty, and the pursuit of happiness.

I can't tell the story of you, America, without telling about the way you began,
with the genocide of millions of Indigenous people. I can't tell the story of us, of
me and you, America, without telling about the brutal enslavement and exploitation of my ancestors bought and stolen from the shores of Africa, where I was
supposed to and should have been born in love. But instead you brought my people
here to be born in your original sin. Now the time has come for me to leave so I
can be reborn, so I can give birth to my freed self, in love.

How could you, America, think you could be blessed? How could you, America, think you could produce beauty from your creation of horror? It is that delusion that is still the most American thing about you, America.

I've spent years spitting and fighting mad at you, trying to fix us, fix this mess you made, trying to change us, trying to make us better, for the kids. Just when I thought I couldn't be angrier or more hurt and disappointed in how you treat us, I was shocked cold with more and more versions of your red-hot blue injustice. When I thought I couldn't be more ashamed of you or when I thought I couldn't be more devastated by your creative and resilient oppression, you somehow managed to surprise me.

And yet what surprises me more is that I still, and always will, love you. For how can I stop loving you after I've been loving you for so long? Despite the disregard and abuse, I will always belong to you regardless of the other countries I travel to, to lay my head down, and fuck to remember, or fuck to forget.

I will always long for you, America. I will always long for more for you, America, and for more for my loved ones who choose to stay. I will always have deep affection for those who remain by choice, or because they have no other choice that they can yet see. I will forever understand the sacrifices made to stay, just as I understand the sacrifices made to leave.

I may get married again eventually. At some point perhaps I'll start paying taxes again. I may even get vaccinated. I'm a human being who can change her mind at any time. But I just needed for the record to show what this relationship has done to me. I needed to see the red, white, and blue truth in Black, white, and gray and, from this place, to decide in what ways I am free and in what ways I will never be, regardless of where I am on the planet.

The question remains, now that I have left: Am I free yet?

I have a lifetime of leaving and loving to answer that. Though I have chosen to leave, I also know that in many ways, deep down, I will always love you.

JOURNAL PROMPT

If you need to write a divorce letter to America, write it.

What Hope

Here is my hope:

I hope that on my deathbed, I am very free and very peaceful, somewhere with open windows, where I can see and hear and feel the Caribbean Sea, surrounded by friends, loved ones, and my children, Adam, Alexis, and Chelsea (who is now one of three Black women judges on the Supreme Court), and their families. My favorite playlist is streaming from the speakers. I am on the other side of many heartbreaks, and I've gotten through and survived seventeen more strains of the COVID-19 virus and another world war.

I imagine it's been fifty years since Trump was assassinated by Putin, and since Biden died of a stroke, making Kamala Harris president, during which time H.R. 40, the reparations bill, was passed and the exploratory committee's findings caused the US government to finally issue a national apology to Africa and her descendants who were enslaved here, and to the generations that followed. They have since been distributing funds to all descendants of Africans who were enslaved from 1619 to the current year of 2074, and reparations also came in the forms of immediate cancellation of all student loan debt, forgiveness of all personal debt and all mortgages, and provision of free healthcare to all US citizens. A law has been passed requiring individuals and corporations making $1 million per year or more to fully fund urban areas all over the nation (excluding the police, of course, who have effectively been defunded).

I hope my eyes close that one last time, after having witnessed more of my people get themselves fucking free.

JOURNAL PROMPT

What freedom do you hope for and fantasize about when you think about your death? What are you going to start doing right now to get there?

ARTIFACT
Activism and Liberation Playlist

1. "Talkin' Bout a Revolution" performed by Tracy Chapman

2. "Get Up, Stand Up" performed by Bob Marley and the Wailers

3. "Bigger" performed by Beyoncé

4. "Changes" performed by Tupac

5. "The Revolution Will Not Be Televised" performed by Gil Scott-Heron

6. "Make It Home" performed by Tobe Nwigwe with David Michael Wyatt

7. "Nobody" performed by Nas with Ms. Lauryn Hill

8. "People of the World" performed by Andre Henry

9. "Black America Again" performed by Common, Stevie Wonder

10. "I Wish I Knew How It Would Feel to Be Free" performed by Nina Simone

11. "They Don't Care About Us" performed by Michael Jackson

12. "What If" performed by India.Arie

Acknowledgments

To everyone who helped bring *AWFY* into the world: To my publisher and friend, Bex, thank you for seeing me and for believing that I had a story worth telling the people and for giving me the opportunity to do that. To my editor, Kristen McGuiness, thank you for doing your Eminem thing with this book. To Dr. Candice Nicole Hargons and Tamela Gordon, thank you for the gift of reading this manuscript and giving me your insight, feedback, and encouragement. And to my writing coach, Kimberly Marsh, thank you for saying hell yes to this book-writing journey with me even before the book deals came. This book would not have gotten written without your consistent support and love; thank you for holding all my words, tears, adventures, and inward-facing language that didn't make the cut.

Thank you to my Jamaica family for helping me get through a year of grieving and healing on those MoBay days and nights: Andre, Delroy, Michele, Judith, and Sonali.

Special thanks to everyone who has been a part of the Legacy Trips family, and to those who helped sustain it while I was focused on writing this book (and living abroad), especially my friend Jen Kinney, Kathi Norman, Susan Andrews, Olivia Bethea, Nya Abernathy, and Lettie Gore.

Deep gratitude to my dear sister friend Trudy Coarde, Dori Koll, and the Holloways, for your friendship and for the space and literal rooms in your hearts and homes that you have allowed me to take up residence in.

And finally, divorce sucks. And it is through the loss, pain, and heartache as an ex-wife that much of this book was written and conceived . . . written by and for the unhealed and unfree parts of myself. Though it filled me with love, offered me lessons and gifts from nature, and connected me to the ancestors and the universe as my teachers and healers, carrying and giving birth to this book broke my heart, but it also put my heart back together and brought me back to life. Getting free means getting healed. I believe that we must be on a healing journey at the same time that we are on our liberation journey (which I am still very much on). It is for this reason that I am extending to and asking myself, my ex-husband, my ex-wife, my friends, my lovers, and my family for grace where my telling of this divorce and liberation story is messy.

Thank you, Jamaica and Costa Rica, for holding me tightly as I wept until I was able to laugh, dance, and remember myself again.

References for
"Honoring the Ori: Mindfulness Meditation at the Intersection of Black Women's Spirituality and Sexualities"
by Natalie Malone and Candice N. Hargons

Afua, Q. (2001). *Sacred woman: A guide to healing the feminine body, mind, and spirit*. One World/Ballantine.

Asanti, I. T. S. (2010). Living with dual spirits: Spirituality, sexuality and healing in the African diaspora. *Journal of Bisexuality*, 10(1–2), 22–30. https://doi.org/10.1080/15299711003760600

Beck, J. R. (2003). Self and soul: Exploring the boundary between psychotherapy and spiritual formation. *Journal of Psychology and Theology*, 31(1), 24–36. https://doi.org/10.1177/009164710303100103

Biggers, A., Spears, C. A., Sanders, K., Ong, J., Sharp, L. K., & Gerber, B. S. (2020). Promoting mindfulness in African American communities. *Mindfulness*, 11(10), 2274–2282. https://doi.org/10.1007/s12671-020-01480-w

Black Girl Bliss. (2018). *Pussy prayers: Sacred and sensual rituals for wild women of color*. Eleven25.

Bojuwoye, O. (2005). Traditional healing practices in Southern Africa: Ancestral spirits, ritual ceremonies, and holistic healing. In R. Moodley & W. West (Eds.), *Multicultural aspects of counseling and psychotherapy series. Integrating traditional healing practices into counseling and psychotherapy* (pp. 61–72). Sage Publications. Ltd. https://doi.org/10.4135/9781452231648.n6

Bullis, R. (1998). Biblical tantra: Lessons in sacred sexuality. *Theology & Sexuality*, 1998(9), 101–116. https://doi.org/10.1177/135583589800500908

Butler, A. D. (2007). *Women in the church of God in Christ: Making a sanctified world*. The University of North Carolina Press.

Carter, R. T. (1991). Racial identity attitudes and psychological functioning. *Journal of Multicultural Counseling and Development*, 19, 105–114. https://doi.org/10.1002/j.2161-1912.1991.tb00547.x

Cole, E. R. (2009). Intersectionality and research in psychology. *American Psychologist*, 64(3), 170–180. https://doi.org/10.1037/a0014564

Collins, P. H. (2002). *Black feminist thought: Knowledge, consciousness, and the politics of empowerment.* Routledge. https://doi.org/10.4324/9780203900055

Crenshaw, K. (2018). Demarginalizing the intersection of race and sex: A Black feminist critique of antidiscrimination doctrine, feminist theory, and antiracist politics. *Feminist Legal Theory*, 57–80. https://doi.org/10.4324/9780429500480-5. (Original work published 1989.)

Day, K. (2018). "I am dark and lovely": Let the Shulammite woman speak. *Black Theology: An International Journal*, 16(3), 207–217. https://doi.org/10.1080/14769948.2018.1492300

Dionne, D. (2020). *Magickal mediumship: Partnering with the ancestors for healing and spiritual development.* Llewellyn Worldwide.

Etta, E. E., Esowe, D. D., & Asukwo, O. O. (2016). African communalism and globalization. *African Research Review*, 10(3), 302–316. https://doi.org/10.4314/afrrev.v10i3.20

Exline, J. J., Pargament, K. I., Grubbs, J. B., & Yali, A. M. (2014). The Religious and Spiritual Struggles Scale: Development and initial validation. *Psychology of Religion and Spirituality*, 6(3), 208–222. https://doi.org/10.1037/a0036465

Gethin, R. (2011). On some definitions of mindfulness. *Contemporary Buddhism*, 12(1), 263–279. https://doi.org/10.1080/14639947.2011.564843

Jones, L. V. (2015). Black feminisms: Renewing sacred healing spaces. *Affilia*, 30(2), 246–252. https://doi.org/10.1177%2F0886109914551356

Jones, L. V., & Harris, M. A. (2019). Developing a Black feminist analysis for mental health practice: From theory to praxis. *Women & Therapy*, 42(3–4), 251–264. https://doi.org/10.1080/02703149.2019.1622908

Kirmayer, L. J. (2015). Mindfulness in cultural context. *Transcultural Psychiatry*, 52(4) 447–469. https://doi.org/10.1177%2F1363461515598949

Moultrie, M. (2018). Putting a ring on it: Black women, Black churches, and coerced monogamy. *Black Theology: An International Journal*, 16(3), 231–247. https://doi.org/10.1080/14769948.2018.1492304

Okello, W. K. (2020). Organized anxiety: respectability politics, John Henryism, and the paradox of Black achievement. *Race Ethnicity and Education*, 1–19. https://doi.org/10.1080/13613324.2020.1798916

Pargament, K. I. & Exline, J. J. (2020, November 1). *Religious and spiritual struggles: Research is shedding new light on an overlooked but important human experience.* American Psychological Association. https://www.apa.org/research/action/religious-spiritual-struggles

Pereira, C. (2016). Frequencies of the Buddhist meditative chant—om mani padme hum. *International Journal of Science and Research*, 5(4), 761–766. https://doi.org/10.21275/v5i4.NOV162732

Richardson, J. L. (2018) Healing circles as Black feminist pedagogical interventions. In O. Perlow, D. Wheeler, S. Bethea, & B. Scott (Eds.), *Black women's liberatory pedagogies*. Palgrave Macmillan. https://doi.org/10.1007/978-3-319-65789-9_16

Sayin, H. Ü. (2017). Tantra, ESR and the limits of female potentials. *SexuS Journal*, 2(3), 55–74.

Somé, S. (2000). *The spirit of intimacy: Ancient teachings in the ways of relationships.* HarperCollins.

Tina's Bibliography

Part One

Stevenson, Bryan. *Just Mercy: A Story of Justice and Redemption*. Melbourne: Scribe, 2020.

Murakawa, Naomi. "Police Reform Works—for the Police," Department of African American Studies, Princeton University. The Trustees of Princeton University, October 26, 2020. https://aas.princeton.edu/news/police-reform-works-police.

Malone, Natalie, and Candice Nicole Hargons. "Honoring the Ori: Mindfulness Meditation at the Intersection of Black Women's Spirituality and Sexualities." *Journal of Psychology and Christianity* 40, no. 2 (2021): 120–27. https://doi.org/10.5040/9781472972835.0225a.

Strawn, Tina, and Jennifer Kinney. "Healing Racial Trauma with Dr. Candice Nicole Hargons." Episode. *Speaking of Racism Podcast* 1. Accessed April 27, 2022. https://www.podbean.com/media/share/pb-qrs5p-f29f44?utm_campaign=w_share_ep&utm_medium=dlink&utm_source=w_share.

An overview of H.R. 40: The "Commission to Study Reparation Proposals for African-Americans Act." Bill. (n.d.).

Emmett Till Antilynching Act. H.R. 55 (2021–2022). https://www.congress.gov/bill/117th-congress/house-bill/55.

Lao-tzu, Gia-fu Feng, and Jane English. "Chapter 15." Essay. In *Tao Te Ching*. New York, NY: Vintage Books, 1997.

Gates, Rolf, and Katrina Kenison. "The Eight Limbs of Yoga." Essay. In *Meditations from the MAT: Daily Reflections on the Path of Yoga*. New York: Anchor Books, 2002.

Part Two

Hanson, Melanie. "Student Loan Debt by Race [2022]: Analysis of Statistics." Education Data Initiative, March 10, 2022. https://educationdata.org/student-loan-debt-by-race.

Hale, Kori. "How Canceling $15 Billion in Student Loans Impacts the Racial Wealth Gap." *Forbes*, February 9, 2022. https://www.forbes.com/sites/korihale/2022/02/03/how-canceling-15-billion-in-student-loans-impacts-the-racial-wealth-gap/?sh=3bb3984618ad.

US Bureau of Labor Statistics. "Average Hours Employed People Spent Working on Days Worked by Day of Week." *Graphics for Economic News Releases*, 2019. Retrieved May 6, 2022, from https://www.bls.gov/charts/american-time-use/emp-by-ftpt-job-edu-h.htm.

US Bureau of Labor Statistics. "Private Industry Workers with Sick Leave Benefits Received 8 Days Per Year at 20 Years of Service." *TED: The Economics Daily*, March 8, 2019. Retrieved May 6, 2022, from https://www.bls.gov/opub/ted/2019/private-industry-workers-with-sick-leave -benefits-received-8-days-per-year-at-20-years-of-service.htm.

US Bureau of Labor Statistics. "Service Requirements for Paid Vacation Leave." *Employee Benefits Survey*, 2021. Retrieved May 6, 2022, from https://www.bls.gov/ncs/ebs/factsheet/paid -vacations.htm.

"Rent Strike." Wikipedia. Wikimedia Foundation, April 22, 2022. https://en.wikipedia.org/wiki /Rent_strike.

Bornstein, Kate, and Laura Erickson-Schroth. "Queer 101: Identity, Inclusion, and Resources." UUA.org, July 20, 2018. https://www.uua.org/lgbtq/identity/queer?fbclid=IwAR0zNsmYq0Fd 7EiLfoscfDpHiEdhqeemObJQrR99BzkwWn_KBblXaUluzyA.

Lorde, Audre. "Uses of The Erotic: The Erotic as Power." Essay. In *Uses of the Erotic: The Erotic as Power*. Tucson, AZ: Kore Press, 2000.

Part Three

"These Three Acts Weaponized Weed against Black Americans." Weedmaps, June 18, 2021. https:// weedmaps.com/learn/cannabis-and-its-evolution/three-acts-weaponized-weed-against-black -americans.

"Alcohol Consumption Is the Sole Cause of 85,000 Deaths Annually in the Americas, Paho/WHO Study Finds." PAHO/WHO, April 12, 2021. https://www.paho.org/en/news/12-4-2021-alcohol -consumption-sole-cause-85000-deaths-annually-americas-pahowho-study-finds.

Part Four

Risen, Clay. "Erica Faye Watson, Comedic 'Hidden Gem of Chicago,' Dies at 48." *New York Times*, March 4, 2021. https://www.nytimes.com/2021/03/04/obituaries/erica-faye-watson-dead -coronavirus.html.

Cheney-Rice, Zak. "Brian Kemp's Fake Crusade for Election Integrity in Georgia." *Intelligencer*, October 16, 2018. https://nymag.com/intelligencer/2018/10/brian-kemp-georgia-election -integrity.html.

Taylor, Keeanga-Yamahtta. Essay. In *How We Get Free: Black Feminism and the Combahee River Collective*. Chicago, IL: Haymarket Books, 2017.

About the Author

———————

Tina Strawn (she/they) is a joy and liberation advocate, activist, author, and the owner and host of the Speaking of Racism podcast and Instagram platform of the same name (IG: @speakingofracism). The heart of her work is leading Legacy Trips (IG: @legacytrips), immersive antiracism experiences where participants visit historical locations such as Montgomery and Selma, AL, and utilize spiritual practices as tools to affect personal and collective change. Tina has three adult children, an ex-husband, an ex-wife, and an ex-country. She has been a full-time minimalist nomad since February 2020. Tina travels the globe speaking, writing, teaching, and exploring where on the planet she can feel safe and free in her queer, Black, woman-identifying body. Connect with Tina at www.tina-strawn.com and on Instagram @tina_strawn_life.